STEP-BY-STEP
CROWDFUNDING

*Everything You Need to Raise
Money From the Cowd*

JOSEPH HOGUE, CFA

Published in the United States of America

ISBN-10 #996232109
ISBN-13 #978-0-9962321-0-4

Joseph Hogue, CFA

Born and raised in Iowa, I graduated from Iowa State University after serving in the Marine Corps. Working with a Canadian venture capital firm, I started talking to small business owners that didn't qualify for the firm's investment criteria about crowdfunding and alternative finance. I have appeared on Bloomberg as an expert in emerging market investing and have led a team of equity analysts for sell-side research.

I hold the Chartered Financial Analyst (CFA) designation, the gold standard for ethical and professional conduct in investment management.

Crowd101.com is your first stop into both worlds of equity and reward-based crowdfunding. Unlike other sites that only offer information for crowdfunding campaigns, on *Crowd101*, you'll find information for investors and supporters as well as for crowdfunding projects.

Contents

How to Use This Book

I am passionate about what crowdfunding can mean for small business and social causes and could talk about it all day, but that's not why you bought this book.

There are 896 books on Amazon right now on the subject of Crowdfunding. If you want to spend hours reading about the history of this new funding source or what it can do for your business, there are plenty of other options.

In Step-by-Step Crowdfunding, I skip all the filler and fancy language to get straight to the point. This book is for people that have decided to crowdfund and just need to know exactly how to do it. You'll see the process from pre-launch to post-campaign wrap, laid out in detail so you don't miss a single point.

Even though the book is set out as a step-by-step approach, there will be some areas that call back or forward to ideas. For example, budgeting your campaign marketing needs is one of the first things you must do but this is nearly impossible without a good idea of what marketing strategies you need to use. The best way to approach this is with a quick read first, noting questions and ideas in the margins.

After that, you'll have a basic idea of how the different steps work together. Then you will be able to read through the book more carefully and put together your campaign.

But first, I need to warn you thatsuccessfully crowdfunding your project may not be as easy as you are expecting. Stick to the process though and you'll not only raise more money than you were expecting but you'll build a loyal community around your business that will carry you on to even bigger things.

What is Crowdfunding?

Small business directory Manta sent a poll to its readers before a webinar on crowdfunding. One of the questions was, "Have you ever or would you consider crowdfunding as a source of funds?"

Less than 3% of respondents answered that they had used crowdfunding in the past and less than 15% answered that they would consider raising funds from the new form of financing. Asked why they would not consider crowdfunding, many business owners responded that they didn't want to be seen as needy by customers, or have customers think that their business was in trouble.

Given the rapid rise of crowdfunding over the years to 2015, this widespread misconception of the funding source really set me back. There are a lot of myths about crowdfunding. Besides the idea that it is only for those in need, most think of it as simply another source of financing.

Raising money through one of the many online platforms can take your business to the next level but it is not the biggest benefit to crowdfunding. Crowdfunding is really about building a sense of community around a product or idea. It is about crowdsourcing your passion and building a crowd around your business.

Six Habits of Highly Successful Crowdfunding

Before we get to the steps you'll use to successfully crowdfund your idea, there are six habits that I see consistently in nearly all great campaigns.

You won't need the typical seven habits to be successful in crowdfunding but you will need to pay attention to these six.

Personal

Successful crowdfunders share with others and have an active social network. They share their emotions and their excitement. Data shows that campaigns where the founder had just 10 Facebook friends, the odds of making a $10,000 funding goal were just one-in-eleven. For founders with 100 friends, the odds jump to one-in-five.

Comprehensive

People think crowdfunding is simply posting a campaign on Kickstarter and maybe tweeting it out to their network. Crowdfunding is so much more. In fact, I know a lot of small business owners that have completely revamped their marketing strategy around crowdfunding. An effective crowdfunding campaign involves offline and online marketing, strategic thinking, logistics, research and outreach. You'll need a comprehensive plan to bring everything together.

Team Builder

Effective crowdfunding means building a team to help you reach your goal. While the project may be your brain-child, realize that it has the potential to be bigger than your, and will benefit from a team effort. One of the biggest surprises crowdfunders run into is the amount of time a campaign can take. The outreach, networking and general administration you will need to do while your campaign is live can easily take 20 hours or more each week.

Slava Rubin, founder of Indiegogo, states that teams raise an average of 70% more money than campaigns run by a single person. Putting together a team of your most passionate supporters helps in two ways. It will bring expertise and skills from the experience of your team and will spread some of the work around so you're not run ragged.

Aggressive

Only your mother is going to help your crowdfunding campaign without being asked. If you are not ready to ask people for help, sometimes asking more than once, then you need to rethink whether crowdfunding is for you.

According to the Public Management Institute, not asking is the single biggest mistake in fundraising. Only about half (56%) of households say they have been asked to give to at least one non-profit, of these, 95% said they gave to at least one.

Creative

There are nearly 8,500 projects right now on Kickstarter alone. A great product will not sell itself and you need to get creative to get people's attention.

About 30% of supporters on Kickstarter are repeat backers, who regularly support multiple campaigns. Asked how they decide which campaigns to support; 27% said they support campaigns that make them laugh, 15% support campaigns that make them think, 42% support campaigns with cool products and 16% support campaigns that evoke other emotions.

Strategic

So much media attention goes to crowdfunding success stories that people don't realize how much goes into an effective crowdfunding campaign. Crowdfunding is not writing out a few words and waiting a couple of months for your campaign to end. You'll need to put together a complete strategy from outreach and building your online presence to the logistics behind fulfilling your reward promises.

Campaigns that raise no money before their launch have an average success rate of just 15 percent. For campaigns that raise just 5% of their goal before launch, the success rate jumps to 50 percent.

Pre-Launch Crowdfunding

The most overlooked stage in crowdfunding is also the most important to the success of your campaign. In your pre-launch activities, you will build the community and the excitement that will carry your crowdfunding campaign though the short period when it is live on a platform.

In fact, you'll notice that 11 of the 17 steps in successful crowdfunding are in the pre-launch stage. Follow this process before you launch your campaign and the actual crowdfunding will be a breeze.

Step One:

SHAPING A SUCCESSFUL CROWDFUNDING IDEA

Putting your crowdfunding idea together is a lot like traditional business planning, but there are some key points you need to build into your plans.

While crowdfunding was seen as an alternative form of finance just a few years ago, it's quickly becoming a viable means of launching your new product or business. While equity crowdfunding generally raises higher sums, even rewards-based crowdfunding has hit amounts in the tens of millions of dollars.

Product, Service or Social Cause

Few campaigns start for the sole purpose to crowdfund something. You've most likely got an idea for a product or service and want to explore ways to raise money. The process of developing your product and business plan is going to be fairly general, but there are some points you'll want to consider when it comes to crowdfunding.

Kickstarter or Indiegogo are generally the go-to decisions for most campaigns, but your product decision will affect which crowdfunding platform will best suit your needs.

- If you plan on selling your product internationally, you may want to go with Indiegogo or another platform other than Kickstarter. While Kickstarter claims to make international crowdfunding just as easy, I have heard from several campaigns that they ran into problems with shipping and collecting pledges.

- Kickstarter may not accept your campaign if it is a social cause, though Indiegogo is more flexible with types of projects. Other platforms like GoFundMe are more focused to social causes and may provide a better environment where backers are looking for projects like yours.

Know your product and your customer

As with any product development or business plan, one of your key questions is going to be the product's unique selling point. What needs does the product satisfy and why does it do it better than existing products? Establishing these needs is even more important ahead of your crowdfunding campaign because understanding those needs will help you reach backers on an emotional level.

Think about your product not in terms of what it does but what it means for customers. A fine ballpoint pen is not just something with which to write but an expression of your thoughts. Buying a quality pen is a symbol of your success and respect for an art form that has died out.

Understanding these needs will help you understand what type of people are most likely to buy your product and support the campaign. Once you have an understanding of this customer segment, you can start to build a picture of their interests and what kinds of things they do online. You won't do much with this yet but will go into more detail to build your crowdfunding outreach list of people to contact before your launch.

Having thought through needs fulfilled by your product and its target customers, you can start developing your sales pitch. There are different thoughts on this but I like having two pitches ready, a very brief 30-second pitch and a longer two-minute proposal.

- Developing your pitch is important for two reasons. Not only will it give you a well-rehearsed lead to grab people's attention but it will also force you to think critically about your product's most interesting aspects.

- The 30-second pitch will be used most often and should hit on no more than two key points. The power isn't really in the details here but in creating enough interest that the person wants to know more. You don't even need to mention the product's name or even what it is in this pitch. Lead with the problem or need with which your market suffers and explain in one sentence how your product will solve it.

- For times when you are asked to explain the product to a group or if your 30-second pitch gets a follow-up question, use your two-minute pitch to fill in the details. Even this pitch isn't meant to answer all questions and should leave enough unanswered questions to have people interested in finding out more. Your two-minute pitch will likely double as much of the script for your primary crowdfunding video.

Vetting your Crowdfunding Idea with Friends and Family

Unless you are already developing your crowdfunding idea with a team, your first interaction with others will be to bounce the idea off of friends and family. They might not have the business savvy or know-how to critique your plans but they will be able to look at it from a customer-perspective.

Your closest personal network will be the most upfront with criticism and you should be able to get some valuable feedback on your product and pitch. While you might have to build a relationship with others on your outreach list before you can get a phone conversation to talk about the crowdfunding idea, your friends and family represent a quick opportunity to get instant feedback.

There are two primary hurdles in crowdfunding, establishing trust and sharing your passion. While friends and family may not share your passion for the product, as might others from affinity groups, you will not have to spend the time to develop a level of trust. If you can find a way to share your passion for the product, you might just find your first crowdfunding supporters in these initial conversations.

Building a Team around Your Crowdfunding Idea

While your crowdfunding idea or product might be your baby, an effective campaign is too much for one person to handle. A crowdfunding campaign can easily require 20 hours per week and much more if you plan on raising more than a few thousand dollars. Not only are other people going to help take some of the workload off your shoulders, but they will also bring ideas and experience to complement your own.

From your conversations with friends and family, you should be able to get at least one or two people that are interested enough to commit a little extra time to be involved. This doesn't have to mean a big commitment but can be as little as spending an hour or two each week to answer emails or perform outreach tasks. Have a few easy tasks in mind to suggest, or talk with them about what they would be best able to do and when.

The idea of recruiting from friends and family first is two-fold. You'll be starting from the level of trust and friendship which will help in securing some kind of commitment. You'll also get the opportunity to practice bringing people closer into the community of your crowdfunding campaign. This practice is going to be important as you start asking for higher levels of commitment from people that may not know you as well.

How Much Will Your Crowdfunding Idea Cost?

Developing a budget for your crowdfunding idea is one of the most important and overlooked steps in crowdfunding. Most crowdfunders include a fairly simple budget in their campaign planning but never go beyond this back-of-the-envelope calculation. Even if their campaign is successfully funded, disappointment sets in when they figure out that they grossly underestimated the costs and the campaign actually ends up costing them money.

Creating a detailed budget for your crowdfunding idea may seem counter-intuitive, especially if your campaign is for a creative project, but it will go a long way to establishing trust and credibility with crowdfunding supporters. The fact that you have taken the time to detail each expense in your project will help show funders that you know the reality of seeing the project through to completion.

If you have never worked with spreadsheets like Microsoft Excel, then now is your chance. Spreadsheets make budgeting much easier than listing everything out on a sheet of paper and you'll be able to detail your budget out further as you get more information. If you need help with basic spreadsheet use, YouTube is a good source for quick tutorials.

Within your budget spreadsheet, you will start with the basic expenses:

- Marketing expenses—Will you need to advertise what your project or business offers?

  - Campaign marketing—Most campaigns don't even think about the cost of their time and the money they spend marketing their campaign. Crowdfunding campaigns are a ton of work, require hundreds of hours and can cost a significant amount in marketing. These costs are all part of your project idea and should be included in your budget.

  - Project marketing—Post-campaign marketing expenses usually get a little more attention in the budget but still not enough. Separate these costs into online and offline expenses. Then these two categories should be further separated into estimated spending on different websites, programs, catering dinner parties, invitations, offline advertising and any other media you need to get your message across.

- Administrative expenses—Office support including supplies, rent, utilities and staffing are all important to show that you will have the resources to make your crowdfunding idea work.

  - A lot of these will depend on how big your project is going to get. No one expects you to run your business out of the garage forever. Even Mark Zuckerberg had to move Facebook out of his dorm room eventually.

- Insurance—Property, health, workman's compensation.

  - Supporters have backed your product and have an interest in seeing it through to the end. You need to protect that interest by protecting yourself against problems that could mean an immediate end to your project.

- Professional fees

  - The crowdfunding idea and campaign might have been your brainchild, but no one expects you to be all things, all the time. If the project is going to grow and really make an impact, it is going to need professional help like graphic designers, technical developers, outreach

    organizers and a myriad of other staff positions.

Beyond these basic expenses, you will need to add others specific to your product.

- Will you need manufacturing facilities or other commercial property?

- Expenses for utilities like phone, water and heat may vary depending on usage.

- Will your product require any licenses, permits or legal filings?

- How much will raw materials cost to produce a sample or first batch of the product?

Rewards and the cost of delivering those rewards are an integral part of your budget. This is where the budgeting can get a little tricky though because you might not know exactly how many of each reward-level will be chosen. Figure out how much it will cost to produce each reward, remembering that you might be able to get volume discounts if you produce in large quantities. Don't forget to add in an approximate cost for shipping each within the United States.

Once you know how much it will cost to produce and ship each reward, you can go one of two routes for a basic idea of rewards fulfillment.

- You can assume that an equal amount of your funding is spread across each reward-level. If you are raising $10,000 and have five reward levels, then each one will bring $2,000 in pledges. From here, you divide the $2,000 into the reward size to find how many of that reward you would need to produce and deliver. Do this across all reward levels and you will get an idea of how much everything will cost.

- A safer method is to assume that all your funding comes at the most expensive reward level. You will take the expenses from producing and delivering the necessary amount of rewards at that level against your funding goal. I like this method because it gives you a worst-case estimate for cost of rewards fulfillment.

- Understand that most crowdfunding campaigns for a product or service are considered a business by the Internal Revenue Service and you'll own income taxes on the project. The accounting is similar to basic business bookkeeping, with the expenses you pay for the campaign offsetting any money you raise. I won't go into every detail of small business accounting but there are a few points you will want to remember.

- If you run your crowdfunding campaign from home, you can write off a portion of your property taxes and utilities as expenses for the campaign as well as any equipment you use. To do this, you calculate the amount of square footage around the space you use. This is the size of the room where you do the work. You then take that square footage divided by the total square footage for your house to get the percentage used for business purposes. This percentage applied to utilities and other household costs can be taken as a business expense against any money raised crowdfunding.

- Keep receipts for all rewards and fulfillment. These will be your primary expenses against the money you raise crowdfunding.

- One stumbling block that gets many crowdfunders at tax time is the fact that money comes in quickly but expenses can take several months or years to build up. The money you raise crowdfunding is considered taxable in the year you received it. Under accounting rules, you can choose to delay the recognition of that money to match it with expenses but you need to know how to show this on financial statements.

After you have selected the crowdfunding platform most appropriate for your campaign, you will have an idea of fees charged to raise the money. Most platforms charge around 5% of the money raised and around 3% for processing the funds. This means dividing the money you need by 0.92 to find how much your goal should be to meet your budget after fees. For example, if you need to raise $1,000 to cover expenses, then you will need to set your goal at $1,087 ($1,000 divided by 0.92) to have $1,000 left over after the 8% fees.

With a detailed budget that includes taxes and fees, you should consider reaching out to other crowdfunding campaigns to check your numbers. Reaching out to other campaigns about costs that you might have missed can save a huge headache later in the process.

Once you have a rough idea for how much your product will cost to launch, you need to make one of the most important decisions in crowdfunding. Too many crowdfunding campaigns reach for tens of thousands of dollars or more to fund years' worth of expenses or the whole production process. The business owner puts in countless hours towards the campaign only to miss the funding goal and receive nothing in the all-or-nothing Kickstarter model.

Instead of trying to fund everything with just one campaign, consider setting your funding goal high enough to reach a milestone like a test product or a draft copy. Nearly three-fourths of Kickstarter campaigns raise less than $10,000 and less than 3% raise more than $100,000 successfully.

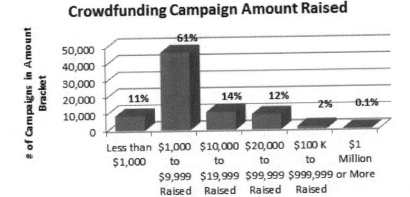

Source: Kickstarter Stats, 2014

My advice would be to set the bar low for your initial crowdfunding campaign, only trying to raise enough that you can provide a working model or something as a reward to backers. With a successful campaign under your belt, it will be much easier to fund successive campaigns since you will already have a base of backers and the experience as a guide.

Setting a Timeline for your Crowdfunding Idea

The final step in putting together your crowdfunding idea is to develop a basic timeline for the project. Some of this will depend on your own deadlines and circumstances but there are a few rules you should remember.

The most important stage of crowdfunding is before your campaign even goes live on the internet. The minimum amount of time you should plan for pre-launch activities is three months. Within three months, you should start seeing visitor traffic coming to your blog from Google search and you will have built a decent mailing list from your outreach efforts. If you have the time, developing your pre-launch following over a longer period like six months can help to raise more awareness and more money.

Studies have shown that shorter campaigns are relatively more effective than longer ones. This is because visitors to your crowdfunding page get a sense of urgency if they see that the campaign is coming to a close within a few weeks. If your campaign has more than 30 days left, some of that urgency is lost and there is no guarantee that visitors will come back later and support your project.

With most of your outreach work done in pre-launch, your biggest days will be the first few after the campaign goes live. In fact, most campaigns start strong before going into a lull until the last week. Besides the sense of urgency created from a shorter campaign, you risk burning out on the continuous work involved in a crowdfunding campaign if you try to raise money over an extended period. Generally, between 30 days and 45 days will give you enough time to drive people to the campaign while not being too long to risk burnout or sap that sense of urgency.

Another often overlooked part in the planning process is building your timeline around production and fulfillment of rewards. There is a growing chorus online from crowdfunding backers that have been disappointed by campaigns that failed to live up to promises made during the campaign. Do not assume that you will never need to come back to the crowd for funding. Even if you never crowdfund another product, crowdfunding backers are some of the most engaged and loyal customers you could hope for. Do not alienate them by grossly underestimating the amount of time it will take to deliver rewards.

Budgeting rewards and fulfillment should give you an idea of how long it will take to deliver them as well. Talk to your suppliers about contingencies for higher quantities of production if you end up blowing away your funding goal. In business, you would plan out three different scenarios for production costs and fulfillment times. You then take the average of the three as a good estimate for worst-, base-, and best-case scenarios.

Once you have an estimate for how long it will take to produce and deliver awards, a good rule of thumb is to increase this amount of time by 20 percent. There is nothing wrong with delivering rewards ahead of schedule but you really do not want to fall behind. If you do start to fall behind in your schedule, be open and upfront with backers. Most will understand and appreciate the regular communication update, especially if fulfillment delays were caused by a much higher funding reached.

Knowing about how long your crowdfunding campaign will take from pre-launch through rewards fulfillment can help to build in a really important idea into the schedule. Try planning your crowdfunding campaign to coincide with a conference or other industry event. Getting a booth or just having a demonstration product on-hand is a great way to showcase your idea and get people to visit your crowdfunding page. Conferences represent a major source of potential backers that you know will be interested in your product.

I've included an example graphic for a crowdfunding timeline below. I assumed general times I've seen in successful campaigns including:

- Shaping an idea (3 weeks)

- Campaign research (2 weeks)

- Campaign outreach (3 weeks)

- Community building (9 weeks)

- Revising the campaign and write-up (1 week)

- Running the campaign (6 weeks)

- Post-campaign fulfillment (5 weeks)

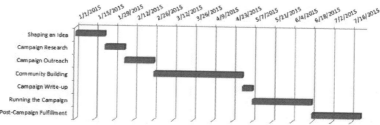

Post-campaign requirements will probably vary the most depending on how much manufacturing you need to do. Understand that you will want to detail out the timeline you post on the campaign page with specific tasks to show supporters that you have built in everything you'll need to do in post-campaign fulfillment.

Crowdfunding Idea Wrap-Up

Putting a crowdfunding idea together isn't something you will be able to do in a short afternoon. Like any good business idea, it will take time to develop, and you will likely be revising the idea well after the early stages of the project. Start off with a quick sketch of each step and then continue to fill in details as more information becomes available.

As with any steps in the crowdfunding process, don't rush this planning stage or generalize any of the details. Planning everything out here will help avoid a lot of hassles and will drive the success of your crowdfunding campaign when it goes live.

Backers will appreciate the fact that you took the time to detail your budget and your rehearsed pitch will pay off through interest from the people you meet.

Step Two:

CHOOSING A CROWDFUNDING PLATFORM

Kickstarter gets more than 13 million visitors to its site every month, followed by Indiegogo with about nine million monthly visitors. These two platforms are usually the number one or two choices for most campaigns but you really should spend a little time on the decision.

There are literally hundreds of crowdfunding platforms. While many of them are probably not worth your time, spend an hour or two researching your options. Smaller platforms may be able to offer one-on-one service and a feature on their homepage, in addition to more targeted traffic.

Included is a list of 18 crowdfunding and fundraising websites that can help you raise money online. Besides fees and the types of projects allowed on the sites, pay attention to which categories seem to do the best. If the site has a forum or some type of community, spend some time to see if it leans toward any particular category or demographic. This will give you an idea of the kind of audience you can expect from the site and how appropriate it is for your campaign.

1)   Kickstarter

The largest crowdfunding site with more than 13 million visitors every month, Kickstarter hosts crowdfunding campaigns from comics and crafts to technology and theater. The site does not allow campaigns for social causes so you'll need a product or event to promote.

The platform has helped nearly 80,000 projects get funded with a strong community of repeat backers. Nearly 300,000 people on Kickstarter have backed 10 projects or more. About the biggest drawback for Kickstarter is that it only offers the all-or-nothing funding model which means that if you do not reach your funding target, you get none of the funds pledged.

Fees:

Kickstarter collects a 5% fee for successfully funded projects. Payments are processed by Stripe, which charges between 3% and 5% of the amount.

2)   Indiegogo

Similar to Kickstarter, except that here, you can raise funds for any project (so long as it's legal), including donations for charity. This opens the crowdfunding site up to campaigns for personal finances, medical needs and just about anything. Kickstarter has gotten better about supporting international campaigns but I still hear from some campaigns that they prefer Indiegogo for raising money from international sources.

The flexibility and ease of international crowdfunding on Indiegogo has helped its popularity and campaign success is slightly higher at 44% compared to Kickstarter. The site receives upwards of nine million visitors per month.

Fees:

Under the flexible funding model, Indiegogo charges a 9% fee on the funds raised. If you reach your goal, you get 5.0% back, for an overall fee of 4%. Fees for the all-or-nothing model are a flat 4% of contributions. PayPal or credit card processing is available with fees ranging between 3% and 5% of the amount.

Indiegogo offers a 25% discount on their platform fees for any campaign raising funds for a nonprofit institution with a 501(c) (3) registration in the United States. Contributions for these campaigns are tax-deductible.

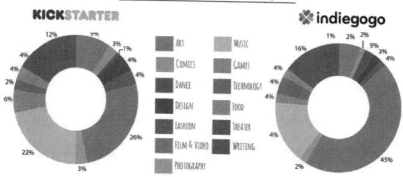

Image courtesy of Simran Khosla at PandoDaily

3)   AngelList

AngelList is a platform for startups to meet investors, candidates and incubators. In the past, angel investing was one of the best forms of funding for startup companies, similar to venture capital, and was typically the first round of funding after friends and family. AngelList is an equity crowdfunding site where companies offer an ownership stake in exchange for funding.

Syndicates—An angel or fund forms a syndicate, picking which investments it likes and wants to support. Private investors then support the syndicate to invest indirectly or directly in the separate projects.

Cost:

For Startups—No fees to receive an investment from a syndicate

For Backers—5–20% carried interest per deal to the syndicated lead and 5% carried interest to AngelList

Self-syndication—Allows accredited investors the opportunity to make direct investment in individual campaigns.

Cost: Investors pay a 10% carried interest to AngelList and a fixed setup cost.

4)   Appbackr

Appbackr aims to index the world's apps, helping developers raise funding and to build attention around their apps and app ideas.

Developers can sign up and post their apps, whether they are still in development or currently for sale in a mobile app store. Backrs purchase wholesale copies on appbackr and makes a 26% profit when he backs an app. If the app is already available, funds are immediately transferred to the developer's PayPal account. If the app is pre-launch, the funds will be available when the app is ready to be released.

As the app sells, appbackr counts the number of sales and pays the developer and the backrs when the mobile app store distributes the money.

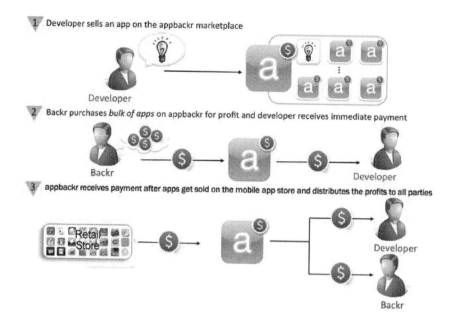

Products

AppBakr has three main products:

- **Appscore**, which provides incentives and rewards to developers based on a ratio between the appscore and its current market performance;

- **Xchange**, which provides a platform to developers to receive offers from stores and platforms to port their apps; and

- **Marketplace**, which has helped developers to crowdfund $1 Million to develop and market their new apps.

5)   RocketHub

RocketHub is one of the more popular sites after Kickstarter and Indiegogo and has a great support system with the crowdfunding site's Success School series. The platform offers the flexible funding model where you keep any pledges made whether you meet the funding goal or not.

RocketHub has partnered with A&E Project Startup for a huge potential boost to campaigns. Campaign owners have the chance to be featured on television and on the A&E website, as well as featured in the channel's bi-annual magazine.

Fees:

If you reach your goal, 4% commission fee + 4% credit card handling fee. Fees for flexible funding if you don't reach your goal are higher at 8% plus the 4% processing fee.

6)   Crowdrise

CrowdRise allows you to create a fundraiser online for your favorite cause. The site runs on the flexible funding model where you keep all pledged donations. The site is one of the largest for social cause crowdfunding and used by some of the largest non-profits including the Red Cross, UNICEF and the Boston Marathon. Crowdrise offers a unique point system that helps track the impact charities are making through their reporting numbers.

CrowdRise offers three pricing plans for crowdfunding:

- The Basic Plan has no annual fee but charges 5% plus credit card fees of 2.9% + $0.30 for each transaction.

- The Featured Plan includes a $49 per month fee but reduces the donation fee to 4% plus credit card fees.

- The Royale Plan charges $199 per month but lowers the donation fee to 3% plus credit card fees.

7)   Fundable

Fundable is one of the few crowdfunding platforms to offer both equity crowdfunding and rewards-based crowdfunding. One of the most interesting features on Fundable is that it charges no fee associated with how much your campaign raises (i.e., the 5% fee on Kickstarter). This means you keep any money pledged and makes the site more attractive to those looking to raise a large amount.

Pricing and Fees:

Fundable charges $179 per month plus a merchant processing fee of 3.5% + $0.30 per transaction for rewards-based crowdfunding.

The site charges $179 per month for equity crowdfunding campaigns.

8)   SeedInvest

SeedInvest is a platform that enables equity-based crowdfunding by accredited investors in startups. Crowdfunding campaigns must reach their funding goal to receive any funds. Companies should expect to take a minimum of 60–90 days to complete equity crowdfunding.

The crowdfunding site charges no investor fees and allows you to invest alongside with institutional investors.

Costs:

—7.5% placement fee, to be charged on the value of the fundraising upon successful completion.

—Between $3,000 and $5,000 in due diligence, escrow, marketing and legal expense reimbursements.

9) WeFunder

WeFunder is another equity crowdfunding site but offers lower minimums for investment. You still have to be an accredited investor but can invest as little as $100 for an individual company.

Startups receive most of the funds committed, minus an admin fee. Investors also pay a $10–$75 admin fee on top of their investment.

Fees:

WeFunder charges 10% carried interest, and a nominal admin fee between $2,000 and $4,000 upon the successful close of the funding.

10) CrowdCube

CrowdCube is a U.K. company backed by Balderton Capital and more than 400 private investors who have collectively invested more than £1.8M across multiple rounds of funding. You can find investment opportunities in a variety of industries or raise funds for your business. Currently, they only support British businesses.

Fees:

Success fee—5% (VAT Exempt) of total funds processed

Administration—£1,250 (ex. VAT)

Corporate services—£1,250 (ex. VAT)

Payment Processing Fees: 2.4% of the funds processed + £0.20 per transaction

11) GoFundMe

GoFundMe is one of the most popular sites for personal fundraising causes. The platform offers a little more personalization in campaigns and three models for fundraising: personal campaigns, charity fundraising and all-or-nothing campaigns.

Under the personal campaign model, you set up your campaign and request donations. This is a good option for those looking to fund medical expenses, memorials, and travel because you don't have to offer rewards. For personal campaigns, you do not have to set a deadline or funding goal.

The charity model allows you to choose one of the non-profit organizations listed on the site and promote it through your social network.

The all-or-nothing campaign model is similar to Kickstarter where you create a crowdfunding campaign and offer rewards for backer contributions.

In the United States, GoFundMe deducts a 5% fee plus a processing fee of about 3% and $0.30 from each donation you receive. International fees range from 6.9% to 7.9% depending on the country. Charities pay a 5% platform fee and a 4.25% fee to FirstGiving.

12) YouCaring

YouCaring offers crowdfunding for personal and charitable causes and charges no fee to fundraising organizations. The site specifically offers categories of medical and healthcare costs, memorial and funeral costs, education and tuition fundraising, family and adoption costs, faith-based service projects, pet and animal expenses, and community or cause.

YouCaring does not permit fundraising for legal defense, litigation, bail bonds or other legal matters.

Fees:

YouCaring does not charge admin or service fees though donors are given the option to donate to the website to support operations. PayPal and WePay offer third-party payment processing and charge 2.9% plus $0.30 per transaction.

13) GiveForward

GiveForward is an online fundraising and donation website that claims to be the number 1 crowdfunding platform to start a medical fundraiser and the only site with fundraising coaches providing guidance. Specific categories include medical bills, veterinarian bills and funeral expenses.

Each fundraiser is assigned a personal coach that is available to answer questions and provide advice via phone or email. Besides the personal coach, an attractive feature is that the fundraising campaign can distribute funds to the recipient any time and in chunks or all at once.

Fees:

Giveforward charges 5% for the platform plus 2.9% + $0.50 goes to their online payment service provider.

14) Patreon

Patreon was launched to enable fans to support their favorite creators and is geared towards ongoing projects of music, video and other creative projects. The site offers a really unique model in that backers pledge to support creators on an ongoing basis, usually for each project, until the backer cancels the promise. Pledges are generally for smaller amounts than the one-time donations on other crowdfunding sites but can grow over time with multiple projects.

Patreon can be a great way for those in the creative space to fund their ongoing projects without having to constantly worry about raising money for each individual campaign. Rewards are offered but are usually only deliverable one time.

Fees:

Patreon charges 5% on pledges with credit card processing adding another 4% off the donation. Beyond these fees, creators also pay billing partners for payment processing between 2% and 5% of the amount.

15)   AlumniFinder

AlumniFunder aims to help build deeper relationships between students and alumni by providing a platform to fund creative and innovative projects within the university community.

People who register on AlumniFunder are divided into two groups: Students and alumni looking to create a project ("Doers") and Alumni and the general public who are looking to browse and fund these projects ("Alumni"). Crowdfunding campaigns run for a limited time (30–60 days) and operate on the all-or-nothing model. As of this writing, there were no active projects listed on the site.

The idea of an alumni networking crowdfunding platform makes a lot of sense as alumni have been strong supporters of campaigns on other sites.

16) AppStori

AppStori is a crowdfunding and fundraising platform connecting mobile app consumers and developers before an app becomes available on an app store.

Developers can raise funds, find beta testers, build an audience, advertise their needs and wants and create a "Stori", essentially allowing friends, family and consumers to be part of the team that brings the app to the market.

When consumers find a team or an app they would like to support, they can make a contribution. Depending on the amount, each team offers different rewards to supporters/backers. Payments are facilitated with Amazon Payments.

Fees:

—AppStori deducts 7% of total collected funds.

—Amazon Payments deduct 2–3% for credit card processing.

17) CircleUp

CircleUp is an equity crowdfunding platform that connects accredited investors with innovative consumer and retail companies. Companies must typically have substantial revenue (> $500,000 annually) or other indicators of potential success and are evaluated by private equity investors before being allowed on the site. Average funding time is between two and three months and funds can be raised through convertible debt or equity. Companies pay a commission to FundMe Securities LLC, a wholly owned subsidiary of CircleUp.

Minimum investment size is $1,000 and up, depending on the offering. There are no fees for investors and your investment is returned if the company fails to meet their target funding.

An interesting feature of CircleUp is the ability to follow "circles" based on an affiliate company, usually a private equity analyst or an investment firm. The affiliate publishes their opinion on deals and investors are allowed to co-invest through a fund managed by the affiliate. Investors pay carried interest to be a part of the fund.

18) CauseVox

CauseVox is another fundraising platform developer with tools to create your own website for online fundraising. The fundraising site tool works similar to WordPress with custom themes and templates available.

At the time of this writing, Causevox was offering development with no monthly fees until you raise $5,000 online. At that point, the site offers three pricing plans:

- Starter plans carry no monthly fee but charge 5% on each transaction and limited features.

- Impact plans charge $49 per month but charge only 4.25% per transaction. Users can develop an unlimited number of fundraising sites and have access to more features.

- Pro plans charge $129 per month and a 4% transaction fee with unlimited sites and full access to features.

Payment processing is available through Stripe or PayPal and will amount to another 3% fee per transaction.

Step Three:

CAMPAIGN RESEARCH: KNOWING WHAT TO EXPECT

Researching a crowdfunding campaign is usually an after-thought for most in their crowdfunding campaign strategy but can help keep you from avoiding the mistakes that keep nearly two-thirds of crowdfunding campaigns from reaching their goal.

Researching your crowdfunding campaign really comes down to two parts: knowing what works and is realistic for campaigns like yours and choosing a crowdfunding platform for your needs. Doing these will help you set realistic goals and put you on the path to a successful campaign.

Making Crowdfunding Research a Part of Your Crowdfunding Campaign Strategy

Assuming you know what you want to crowdfund, your first step is to find out how that type of crowdfunding campaign does on different platforms. They best way to do this is to look for previous campaigns that related to your idea. It can take a couple hours searching on the internet and in forums but you'll get tons of information for your time.

If your crowdfunding campaign is for a specific type of product then just Google search, "Kickstarter [product type]" or "crowdfunding campaign [product type]." You could also try replacing "Kickstarter" with Indiegogo or a few other large platforms like RocketHub or GoFundMe. Beyond a basic Google search, you'll want to ask around related online forums for previous campaigns.

The idea is to find at least a few successful projects and a few unsuccessful projects that are very similar to your own. You're going to study these campaigns.

- How much were they trying to raise?

- How many backers did they eventually get and how much did each pledge on average?

- What rewards did they offer?

- How did their video look?

- Were they effective in sharing their passion for the product or cause?

- How did they connect with people on an emotional level?

- Did they lay out their budget and timeline clearly?

- Do they have a website or blog for the crowdfunding campaign?

The easiest course is just to contact the campaign owner directly. I've had pretty good success with this in the past, getting replies from a little over half of prior campaigns. You'll be surprised how willing people are to talk and help out, especially if your campaign is related to theirs.

- You'll want to ask them how they answered the questions above and any challenges they faced during their crowdfunding campaign.

- Check out Kicktraq for the project or ask the campaign owner if they have any analytics they could share. Kicktraq is a neat tool for seeing daily progress in a crowdfunding campaign's funding and seeing what worked in promotions. That big spike in funding on one particular day might be worth checking out to see what they did.

- What forums or groups did the campaign owner get involved with to promote the project? Where any particularly effective?

- You might want to develop a relationship over a few calls or emails but you might even be able to get a list of backers or people that were really passionate about the campaign. Finding an influencer or someone that is willing to put in a couple of hours to help promote your campaign is worth more than money, so don't be shy about asking. The campaign owner may even be willing to help out a little.

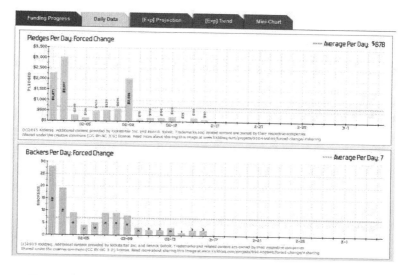

Kicktraq will also show you how many social shares the campaign got, which can be useful in determining which social networks are best for your campaign and how it translates into visitors and backers.

The update and comments section of a crowdfunding campaign page can give you a lot of great information about how the campaign was going and how they dealt with the progress. Beyond going right to the campaign owner, this is the best place to get tips on campaigns similar to yours.

Typing the name of a crowdfunding campaign into Google can help find any promotional activities they accomplished including blogging, forum posts and press. This should give you a few ideas on websites or forums that could be receptive to getting a post by you about your campaign.

One of the best ways to research Twitter is through Topsy. Copy the URL address of the crowdfunding campaign page and put it in the search bar on the Topsy site. It is going to show you everyone that has linked back to that campaign page.

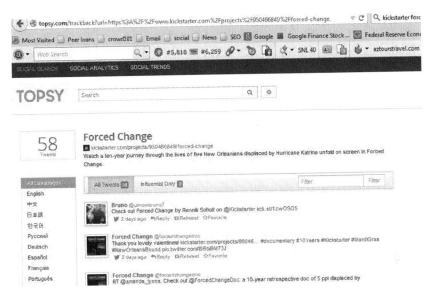

Once you're done researching previous crowdfunding campaigns, you should have a pretty good idea of what you're up against with your own campaign. You'll know specific challenges to the type of campaign and how well it is received on social media. You should also have a good start on your outreach list for influencers and others passionate about your crowdfunding campaign topic.

Step Four:

SETTING REALISTIC CROWDFUNDING GOALS

The most common questions I get from crowdfunding campaigns are, "How much can I raise?" and, "How do I set realistic crowdfunding goals?" While there are no hard-and-fast rules for every campaign, there are some good rules of thumb to follow to help make your crowdfunding campaign a success.

Setting a Realistic Crowdfunding Campaign Budget

Coming from the investment industry, I'm often amazed that people put so much thought into marketing and the write-up for their crowdfunding campaign but fail to really think about how much they need.

Your crowdfunding campaign budget needs to be as detailed as possible in order to set realistic crowdfunding goals, not only to know how much you need but to show supporters that you've put some time thinking about all the costs.

- Include both campaign and project **marketing expenses**—Are you going to need to advertise your product or service after the campaign? While you can crowdfund without spending anything on advertising, it helps to have a budget for campaign outreach.

- **Administrative expenses**—Crowdfunding can be a ton of work and it may be cost effective to hire someone to do routine jobs. Don't forget to include a budget for any supplies, rent and utilities for your campaign.

- Budgeting for **rewards fulfillment** means not just packaging and shipping expenses but budgeting for your time as well.

- **Platform fees** are the most common expenses that get overlooked by campaigns. These can approach nearly 10% of the money you raise, so pay attention to the fine print on the crowdfunding platform.

Once you've budgeted out all your expenses, I would normally recommend you increase it by 10% for miscellaneous expenses and surprises. Crowdfunding is hard enough but running out of money before you fulfill your campaign promises will make it even harder to raise any more money in follow-up campaigns.

Reality meets Budget Needs

After you've put together a detailed budget for your project, it's time for a reality check. Sure, the Star Citizen video game campaign raised $2.1 million but what are your chances?

Of the 76,931 successfully funded projects on Kickstarter, 72% of them raised less than $10,000 and only 85 have raised the legendary $1 million or more. The graphic below shows just how tough it is to raise the big bucks in crowdfunding.

The good news is that if you can raise at least 20% of your goal, odds are that you can reach fully funded. Nearly four-fifths (79%) of the campaigns on Kickstarter that raised more than 20% of their target ended up being successfully funded.

There are two important tips when deciding how high to set your crowdfunding campaign goal:

- If possible, try an initial campaign where you just raise money for idea development. Raise money for market research, legal filings and development of a prototype. This will give you a much lower target at which to aim and will be easier to fund. You'll also have a successful campaign to show potential supporters in follow-up campaigns and you will learn a ton about what it takes to run a successful crowdfunding project.

- Let your pre-launch success help determine your crowdfunding campaign goal. Campaigns that raise no money before their launch have an average success rate of just 15 percent. For campaigns that raise 5% of their goal, the success rate jumps to 80 percent. Raising funds pre-launch helps to show social proof that people already trust you and the campaign. Try raising money for a month before the campaign. Setting your funding goal at less than 20 times the amount you raised pre-launch means you'll start with a good chunk already funded.

Crowdfunding platform Seedrs reports on its blog that once a campaign reaches 30% of its funding goal, the odds of success jump to 90% compared to just a 50% chance across all campaigns.

More than Money

The success rate for projects on Kickstarter is 39% so your biggest goal is probably just going to be reaching your funding target. There is another important goal you should consider for your campaign, traffic and outreach for your project.

One of the biggest benefits to crowdfunding is the marketing exposure you can get for your business or cause. Nearly 15 million people visit the Kickstarter website every month, potentially leading hundreds or thousands to your business.

The crowdfunding platforms don't release statistics on the average number of visitors to a campaign. I've talked to just over 40 crowdfunders since I have been running the blog and the average seems to be somewhere around 2,000 views and a conversion rate of around 5% of those that actually end up supporting a campaign.

Other data shows that the size of your social network is related to the odds of your success in crowdfunding. For campaigns where the founder had just 10 Facebook friends, the odds of making a $10,000 funding goal were just one-in-eleven. For founders with 100 friends, the odds jump to one-in-five. Of course, this doesn't mean start adding random people to your Facebook friend list but be an active engager of others on social media.

Setting traffic goals can help you focus your marketing efforts and really get the most benefit out of your campaign. Work on your social reach before launching the campaign. Engage with people already in your social network and try to reach at least 100 active contacts across the different social media websites.

After launching your campaign, set weekly visitor goals for the campaign page. Most crowdfunding campaigns start really strong but then momentum fades after two weeks. Aim for around 1,000 visitors during the first ten days of your campaign and 750 during the second ten days.

You will want to adjust your goals depending on your funding goal. For example: The average amount from a supporter is around $75, so you will need about 70 backers to meet a $5,000 funding goal. If you can convert 5% of the visitors to your campaign into backers, then you'll need about 1,400 visitors over the life of the campaign.

Your funding target and traffic goal are just two of the milestones you'll want to set for your crowdfunding campaign. What other goals have you set for your campaign? Please use the comment section below or drop me a note on setting goals.

Step Five:

A CROWDFUNDING REWARDS STRATEGY TO BEAT YOUR GOALS

Giving away crowdfunding rewards to reach your crowdfunding goal seems counter-intuitive, especially if your project is a creative work where you really don't expect much return.

The fact is that a smart set of rewards is key to meeting your funding target. Many backers on crowdfunding platforms are there looking for innovative products and gear. To them, it's great that they can support a small business and help you meet your goal but the reward is really the kicker.

In fact, using a system of stretch rewards and goals can help you virtually guarantee you get funded and can help to blow away your initial target.

Crowdfunding Rewards Basics

Crowdfunding rewards are not really rewards in the sense that you are giving something away in a contest. Crowdfunding rewards are more like products, services and special recognition you sell in exchange for people contributing to your campaign.

Setting up a system of reward levels, where the lowest level begins around $1 or $10 and the highest level reaches into the thousands, helps to incentivize people of all economic means and passion for your project. Crowdfunding rewards at the lower levels are going to be trivial items like a thank you, a t-shirt or a digital copy of your work. Making the reward levels cumulative, meaning that each level earns the previous rewards as well, can help incentivize people to contribute to one higher level than they might otherwise.

In a study of more than 200 campaigns, I found campaigns with as few as three rewards and as many as 20 reward levels. Three is way too few reward levels but you also don't need as many as twenty initial reward levels. The average across all the campaigns was 12 reward levels with a median of nine levels.

The more creative you can get with your crowdfunding rewards, the more you will interest random visitors to your crowdfunding campaign page. We'll get to some of the more creative ideas in the next section but a good general rule on crowdfunding rewards is as follows:

- Contributions of $10 or less will get a personalized thank you by email or snail mail. You may also include them in the credits for a video production.

- Contributions of between $10 and $25 may get a digital version of the work or an invitation to a special event.

- Contributions of between $25 and $50 may get a VIP invitation to your event, printed and digital versions of the work or special signed memorabilia.

- Contributions of $100 or more might get special recognition on the work, multiple copies of the work to use as gifts or even an interview or lunch with the campaign owner or cast.

I've seen a lot of crowdfunding reward levels starting at $10 recently, whereas the $1 level was typical in prior years. Starting your rewards at a higher level is tempting, but $10 may be a little high for some casual backers, especially for a minor thank-you reward. I usually recommend starting crowdfunding reward levels at $5 and work up from there.

Getting Creative with Crowdfunding Rewards

Crowdfunding social causes lends itself well to creative and emotional rewards. Your goal throughout the campaign page will be to strike an emotional tone and make people passionate about the cause. This will allow you to make your crowdfunding rewards less costly, emotional-type branding, something that the backer can wear or use to say, "I'm important to this cause."

For these emotional-type crowdfunding rewards; t-shirts, buttons and digital buttons work well. For digital buttons, make sure you show contributors how to post them in their email signatures.

For other crowdfunding campaigns, your rewards will really help drive contributions. If backers see that you are getting something out of the campaign, like funding a product or project, they are going to want something as well.

The lower-level crowdfunding rewards will still be fairly basic for these campaigns but you need to get creative to draw higher-level contributions. Some great ideas I've seen are the following:

- Grant naming rights to characters in your story or production to backers.

- Signed memorabilia by cast or writers, especially if the memorabilia is limited.

- Big money contributors may get parts as extras in the production or a character written after them.

A Crowdfunding Rewards Strategy to Blow Away your Funding Goal

We've already touched on your basic reward strategy and some ideas for creative rewards. You're just a few ideas from really beating your crowdfunding goal.

Limited time or quantity crowdfunding rewards are a good way to build on that sense of urgency within crowdfunding. The most often used of these is limited quantity rewards, giving backers an early-bird offer to get some of the most sought after rewards. Limited-time rewards work best after you've built out a list of backers and community so you can email out the offer.

Add-on crowdfunding rewards is an upsell idea you can pitch to current backers and can be a great way towards the end of the campaign to get that last bit of funding to put you over your goal. The idea is that you contact your current backer list or even your outreach list and offer an add-on reward for backers of a certain reward level. The idea works best if it is for a limited time as well.

While it may not necessarily be a reward, promoting a **limited-time backer pledge** is a powerful way to reinvigorate your campaign. You first need to find a few backers or a new donor that is willing to offer a special reward or match pledge for a limited time. You then promote the match pledge or reward out through current backers and through social networks—Today only! 100% Matching on All Pledges!

My favorite crowdfunding rewards strategy is the stretch goal. The idea is that you set an initial funding goal that is well within reach but will still allow you to develop your product or idea, and then make a set of progressively higher funding goals that will allow you to do extra things for your idea.

Game-maker Cryptozoic Entertainment has worked stretch goals perfectly and raised more than seven-times and three-times their goal in two Kickstarter crowdfunding campaigns. Each stretch funding goal is well within reach of the previous one and includes a special incentive like a new character piece or feature to the game. Read through the updates of the game-maker's campaign and you'll see how they really build excitement for backers to reach that next funding goal. A story is built around each level and the campaign reaches out through social media and the community to build excitement.

Crowdfunding rewards do not have to be expensive or a distraction to your campaign. Besides offering a lot of incentive to backers, they can really help to add features to your product or project. Building out a smart crowdfunding rewards strategy will help you blow your crowdfunding goal out of the water and keep momentum going in your campaign.

Outreach: Reaching an Audience and Influencers

While a lot of your crowdfunding support will still need to come from your existing network, real campaign success depends on your ability to reach out and build a sense of community around the project. This begins with campaign research but the real test is here in the outreach phase of pre-launch crowdfunding.

It's during outreach that you are going to make the initial connections with potential backers, cheerleaders and the all-important influencer.

- Outreach starts with a simple introduction and building out your list of people that might be interested in the campaign.

- Depending on your crowdfunding campaign timeline, you will need to decide how quickly you convert outreach candidates into supporters.

- Start with smaller requests like advice and social shares of your blog posts to bring people into the campaign and build a sense of community.

- Building community with outreach candidates is not a one-way street so be prepared to offer up a little time of your own for their needs as well.

- Do not think that support starts and stops with financial backing. Get to know the people on your outreach list to understand where they can help the most. Offering multiple opportunities to support the campaign will make it easier for them than simply asking for financial support or nothing

Friends and Family

Reaching out to friends and family will be your first task in crowdfunding outreach for a few key reasons. Your closest personal network is probably going to be your strongest supporters, even if they do not share your passion for the idea. Besides their support, they are also likely to be brutally honest with you in offering critique and advice for the campaign.

Within your list of friends and family, you'll have an idea of which will want to help or might be able to offer advice. You'll want to personally contact those with particular experience or that you're sure will want to be active in the campaign. For the rest, I would still recommend sending an email to ask if they would be interested in hearing more about the campaign. Don't write anyone off before you give them a chance.

Your goal should be to get at least one or two people from your closest network to be a part of your campaign team. Even if it's an informal team, you are going to need all the help you can get with outreach and community building. Don't just ask them to help out on an ad hoc basis. Since they might not be as enthusiastic about the campaign, they will need direction on specific tasks. Talk about what they are good at and one specific task they might be able to handle on a weekly or monthly basis. Defining the task in time and process will go a long way in getting their help, especially if it only takes a few hours a month.

Of course, so much the better if you can find someone among your friends and family that is as passionate about the campaign as you. They can take a more active role in the campaign and take a lot of weight off your shoulders.

Reaching out to Previous and Current Campaigns

While researching previous campaigns can give you a ton of information around which to design your own crowdfunding campaign, it can also provide one of the best ready-made outreach networks. Previous crowdfunding campaign owners have already built their network and searched for the best places for their online presence. Because crowdfunding evolved around the idea of helping each other, campaign owners are usually willing to share their experience and may even want to help further.

If you did not contact previous campaign owners in your crowdfunding research, you'll want to do it now. **If you are shy about reaching out and talking to strangers, put down this book and forget about crowdfunding.** Only your mother is going to help your campaign without asking. Most others will have to be asked and sometimes asked multiple times.

Send a brief introduction email telling them that you saw their campaign and were impressed by some of its ideas. You can mention that you are thinking about launching a campaign but you don't need to go into detail. Here you are only asking for 15 minutes to pick their brain about their experience.

If you get a phone call, make sure you are ready to talk about their campaign. Be honest about how you came across their campaign, it will help lead in to your own campaign. Depending on how long they have available you want to try for the following information:

- Is there any topic-specific advice they learned while crowdfunding (i.e., anything that might relate to your product or service)?

- Did they find any social groups on Facebook or LinkedIn that is related to the topic and yielded some good interest from members?

- Did they find any online forums or websites that were particularly helpful?

- Did they find any blogs or bloggers that were receptive to guest posts or talking about the campaign?

- Did they find any journalists or publications that were interested in hearing about the campaign?

You can ask about general crowdfunding and marketing but their real value is going to be in the advice they can offer that's relevant to your industry or topic. You are also going to want to gauge their enthusiasm for the topic and how willing they might be to help you out in your campaign. You don't need to be too aggressive right now; you're only building your outreach network. Follow the phone call with an email thanking them for their time and let them know you will be watching for any of their future campaigns.

Follow the phone call up a week later with another call, asking for a relatively easy favor, like tweeting or passing a blog post of yours through their social network. Not only will this open up their social network to your campaign but you are also furthering your relationship with the crowdfunding campaign owner. Thank them for everything and let them know that you want to help them out as well.

At this point, you should have an idea of what they are doing and possibly something with which they might need help. If you have no idea, just ask. Be generous with your time and try to offer something more than a social share of their webpage or blog post. The back-and-forth here is not just a game though to get a little more out of them for your campaign. If your campaigns are truly related in the same topic, you should be able to find ways to help each other out now and in the future.

It takes some sleuthing but comments may also be a source for your crowdfunding outreach campaign. By clicking on the comments link in a Kickstarter campaign, you can see notes left by backers including other projects they've backed. Kickstarter also provides a neat little pie chart denoting the categories they back most.

The page won't have any contact information but you might be able to find something from a Google search. You might also ask for a personal introduction from the campaign owner, again only after you've established a level of trust. If you are able to contact the backer, just mention that you noticed they back similar projects and were hoping to get their feedback on your upcoming campaign.

The above process is similar with current crowdfunding campaigns though the campaign owner may not be willing to talk about current backers. A lot of crowdfunding campaigns set up reciprocal donations with other campaigns. It is usually at the lowest level of support but can still show that numerical-level of social proof. I wouldn't commit too much though, especially if your campaign has not launched yet.

Online Forums

There are two types of forums on which you will want to focus, forums related to your crowdfunding campaign's category and those related to crowdfunding in general. Forums are a great tool for outreach because they attract exactly the kind of people you need for your campaign. If someone is passionate enough about a topic to spend their time in a forum, they may be willing to spend their time on your campaign.

To find a forum related to a topic, search in Google for [Forum: your topic]

For example, if you were looking for forums about pottery, you would type [Forum: pottery] but without the brackets.

Check out a few forums for how many members they have and how active the community is in discussions. You will probably only have time for maybe two or three forums. Remember, real social networking is about building relationships and offering something of value. You cannot expect to drop a message off on a forum and have people come looking for you.

Introduce yourself on the forum and talk a little about your campaign or idea. Look through other posts and answer questions or relate to others' stories. As with a lot of the social media and outreach tasks here, you will want to schedule out 20 minutes or so each week to come back to the forum and contribute. Do this for a few weeks and you will begin to build a network. Within this network you can start talking a little more about your project and start asking for advice and support. Keep it simple at first, asking for social shares or ideas on contacts with influencers.

Forums dedicated to crowdfunding in general can also be helpful but you have to make sure not to overdo it. Check out a couple of forums and bookmark them if they seem particularly helpful. Spend half as much time on these as you do the forums related to your campaign topic. You might be able to draw some backers from these or pick up some good advice but your focus should be people on other forums that are passionate about your specific campaign topic.

Social Media

Social media can be extremely frustrating for crowdfunding campaigns. While everyone knows it's a pipe dream, there is still that little voice in the back of your head that says, "Maybe my campaign will go viral." After spending tens of hours crafting a social media strategy, low social shares of your campaign can be nearly unbearable.

Understand that click-through rates, or the percentage of recipients that open and click on a link, for email are between 1% and 5% depending on your industry. The rate for social media is even lower, around 0.4% to 0.8% for Facebook and Twitter. Even if people share your post on their social profile, they may not click through and actually look at the campaign.

Before you get too discouraged, there are ways to improve the response to your social media posts. It begins with finding the people that are most likely to share your posts in the first place, those affinity groups that share a passion for the topic. There are two parts here, joining any pages or groups that revolve around the topic and adding people within these groups as friends.

In **Google+** these are known as communities and can be found in the drop-down menu on the left of your Google+ page. Once you are in the main communities page, you can search, join or create a community of your own. It's important to get a feel for each group before you start submitting posts of your own. Check out the group rules (if any) and look through a few posts.

In **Facebook**, you will look for group pages. An important distinction here is to be made between a group and a page. Facebook pages are like personal profiles but for an entity. Your crowdfunding campaign should have its own page. Facebook groups are supposed to be affinity groups set up for communication around the common interest.

As with other outreach groups, try out a few Facebook groups to get the feel for how helpful they might be. A lot of groups will degenerate into worthless spamming if the moderators are not present. Find a couple of groups where people share valuable insight and opinions and start building your presence.

With your group participation, it isn't about reaching everyone in the group but building a relationship with a few members. Since these people are already passionate about the topic, they are likely to be part of a wider social network around the idea and more willing to help you with the campaign. As opposed to the general population where you will need to build trust and passion for the campaign, here you will only need to build trust.

Twitter does not offer a group function but you can create lists that will work in a similar way. When you tweet, you can tweet only to the list or to your general profile page. You can also decide if list members' tweets go to your general page or only to the list. There isn't the same sense of community in Twitter lists but it does provide a way of separating the tweets into specific groups.

- Click on the Lists tab on your profile page and create a list.

- You can add people to your list, share a list with others and request to be added to lists.

- Through the tweets you see from people on topic-related lists, make a note of common hashtags and other Twitter profiles.

I have used **Pinterest** for driving visitors to my blog and there are some good outreach opportunities as well. Searching for your topic will show pins, pinners and boards. Pinners with a lot of followers on Pinterest are likely to have a lot of followers in other social networks and may have their own website. Add a few of these to your list of influencers to contact and follow the strategy below.

Journalists and the Fourth Estate

Journalist and traditional media contacts are like the Holy Grail for crowdfunding. Getting your campaign on the news or in a widely published periodical can mean tens of thousands in donations and an army of backers.

There are two things to remember for getting journalists to cover your campaign, the story and who is most likely to want it.

Your first step is researching which journalists or publications are most likely to be interested in your story. This is usually fairly simple and just a matter of noting the journalists that frequently write about a topic. After all your other research into your campaign, you will likely have come across at least a few names that keep popping up. Even if your campaign is not locally-focused, you will want to note which local journalists cover the topic as well.

The second part of getting journalist coverage is creating a story that others will want to hear. The best way to do this is by relating your campaign to a current event. Can you relate your campaign to a holiday or special community event? Does it relate to a social cause that is making the news lately? You'll have to be fast when reaching out to journalists. Most will source and outline an article days or even weeks in advance of an event.

There are a few resources online for connecting with journalists. The most popular is Help a Reporter Out (HARO), a website set up to connect journalists with informational sources. HARO used to be more helpful in landing journalist contacts but is now pushing its fee-based services pretty heavily. It's still worth filling out a profile and checking in on the site once a week to see if you can find journalists looking for your particular story. Other sites include PressRush, ProfNet, and SourceBottle.

Prioritizing your List and Reaching Influencers

Spend any time on outreach and you are likely to build quite a list very quickly. We talked about the concept of influencers briefly in the blogging chapter but it's worth repeating here. There are some people that are just naturally sociable or that carry huge social networks. You shouldn't neglect anyone that is willing to help your campaign but the most efficient use of your time is going to be spent reaching out to these people.

This is really where your team comes in handy. If you can get a couple of people passionate about the campaign, they can help build outreach with general contacts while you concentrate on influencers. Outreach is tough work so you might want to offer a little something to persuade people to help out. A small stipend or even dinner can go a long way to buying yourself some of their time. The important thing is that they share your passion and will share that passion when reaching out to others.

Prioritizing your outreach list is relatively simple. Websites like Alexa and Compete.com can be used to measure the popularity of another website or blog. For individuals, you can check out how many people are in their social networks on Facebook, LinkedIn and Twitter. Make sure you check out how engaged their social followers are through comments on their social shares.

With website and social measures at hand, you can list the people in your outreach list by how much influence they might have on other people. Besides prioritizing your list in this way, you might also want to highlight the names of people that you know to already be enthusiastic about helping your campaign. Even if they are not particularly influential, there is no sense neglecting what could be some great help.

The people with thousands of active social followers and a highly trafficked website are going to be at the top of your list. Unfortunately, you are not the only person trying to reach out to these influencers. It will take longer to build a relationship and trust with these people before you ask them to be a part of the campaign or to share your project with their network. As we talked about in the chapter on building a crowdfunding blog, this is done through reading, sharing and commenting on their own online material.

You will need to decide the time and effort you commit to different levels of people on your outreach list. For the people toward the bottom of the list that may not be of much influence, a simple email might suffice. In my experience, you are likely to get a response from about 10% of the people that you email without any prior relationship building. Setting up a relationship through a couple of social shares and comments can boost the response to 15% or 20% after a couple of weeks.

Step Seven:

CREATING A CROWDFUNDING CAMPAIGN BLOG

Blogging can be one of the most rewarding activities in your crowdfunding campaign strategy but it can also be one of the most difficult and uncertain. At times you'll feel like you're talking to yourself, but done right, you'll have the potential to drive thousands of people to your campaign page.

But this chapter isn't about convincing you to start a blog for your crowdfunding campaign. For any small business, an online presence should be a given. Even for smaller, one-time campaigns, you will need a way to build support before you launch your campaign.

As someone with two blogs, I can tell you that blogging can be extremely easy or extremely frustrating.

Frustrating if you are not patient and need fast traffic growth while having to learn everything yourself. Reading through this chapter, you'll get an idea of just how much has to come together for a successful blog. Now imagine that you had to search and research all of it yourself like I did. It can take a ton of time.

Blogging for your crowdfunding campaign can be easy though if you build a strategy around a simple process of what works. And that is where we'll begin.

Starting a Blog for your Crowdfunding Campaign, a Complete Guide

There will be three stages to your crowdfunding campaign blog: creating the blog itself, bringing visitors to your blog and using that visitor traffic to support your crowdfunding campaign. Notice here that I am assuming you already know your target audience, who is most likely to be interested in and support your campaign. This chapter is just going to be about blogging. If you haven't done the research around your audience or crowdfunding campaign yet, you will in another chapter.

Creating a Crowdfunding Campaign Blog

Your first job in creating a blog for your crowdfunding campaign is to pick a **domain name**, which is the name of your website. If you've already got a website, this part is already done for you. If not, remember a few things:

- Stick with the standard .com name unless you run a charitable organization, in which case .org works just as well.

- Check out a search site like Instant Domain Search to make sure your site name is available or to get ideas on a name.

- If your "perfect" domain name is taken, try adding things like "a", "the," or "my," but I would stay away from hyphens.

- Simple and easy to remember is the key. Take your time because it is very difficult to change your domain once you've already got things running.

Next you will need to choose a **web host** for your site which will store your site on its servers and provide support. I have used

GoDaddy with another site but was not happy with the features provided. I use BlueHost for this site and my personal finance blog, PeerFinance101.

BlueHost offers a pretty simple installation process and an easy-to-understand platform. Along with different levels of service to fit your needs, they offer a money-back guarantee if you're not happy. The standard pricing is $5.99 per month but click through to one of the links here and you'll get the special offer of $3.95 per month for 36-months plus a free domain name and unlimited email accounts.

I use the "Plus" service since I run more than one site. If you are only planning on running one site, then you'll probably be fine with just the starter service.

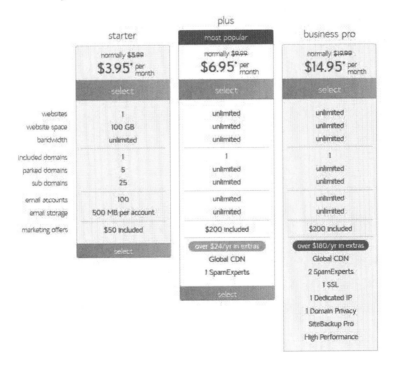

	starter	plus	business pro
		most popular	
	normally $5.99	normally $9.99	normally $19.99
	$3.95 per month	**$6.95** per month	**$14.95** per month
	select	select	select
websites	1	unlimited	unlimited
website space	100 GB	unlimited	unlimited
bandwidth	unlimited	unlimited	unlimited
included domains	1	1	1
parked domains	5	unlimited	unlimited
sub domains	25	unlimited	unlimited
email accounts	100	unlimited	unlimited
email storage	500 MB per account	unlimited	unlimited
marketing offers	$50 included	$200 included	$200 included
	select	over $24/yr in extras	over $180/yr in extras
		Global CDN	Global CDN
		1 SpamExperts	2 SpamExperts
			1 SSL
		select	1 Dedicated IP
			1 Domain Privacy
			SiteBackup Pro
			High Performance

The signup is pretty self-explanatory. You'll fill in your account information and chosen domain name. You will be asked if you want a whole bunch of other products like site backup, site protection and others. I would just start out with the basic package and uncheck all these add-on services. You can add them later if you need them.

After you are done, you will be given a link to the BlueHost homepage where you will login to your hosting account or to your email. I suggest bookmarking this URL and adding it to your favorites at the top of your computer screen. You are going to be using the site a lot so might as well have it handy.

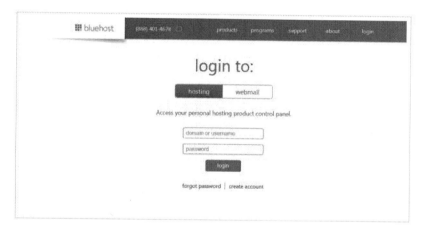

Once you login to your hosting account, you will click on "Install WordPress" under the Website section of the main screen. WordPress is the site builder you will use and where you will manage all the behind-the-scenes stuff for your site. Don't be intimidated by all the buttons and choices on the screen, you'll likely never use many of them.

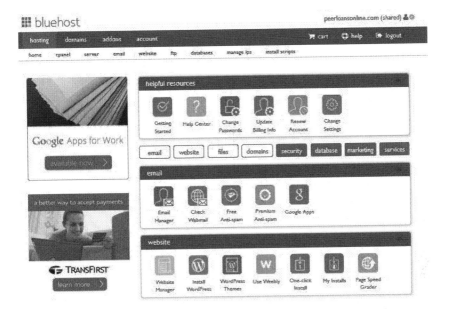

The process to install WordPress is pretty easy as well. You'll enter your domain name and create login information. When the installation is complete, click "View Credentials" to see the website address where you will access WordPress for your blog. This URL, something like **http://www.yourblogname.com/wp-admin,** is very important and you should bookmark it as well.

Once you login to WordPress is when the real fun begins. Within Wordpress is where you will start to build your blog. Along the left-hand side of the screen you will see your menu.

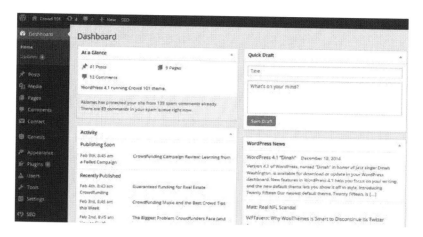

You first need to set up your blog details under the "Settings" item. Fill out your site name, a catchy tagline, and your contact email. Under the settings menu, you will see other sub-menu items. The great thing about WordPress is that a lot of the background stuff is already filled out and you really only need to change a few things.

- For permalinks, I would check the Month and Name setting to help avoid problems with duplicate post titles

- Check out all the sub-headings just to get a feel for where things are in case you want to change something in the future.

The look of your blog is called a Theme, and you can find different ones under the "Appearance" menu item. WordPress offers several options for free and most people will be fine with one of these. I use a premium theme from a private provider called StudioPress, one of the most popular theme developers. Buying one of these themes will cost a little more but it comes with extra features and can really make your blog stand out. I like the magazine themes because they offer a lot of places to highlight posts.

Once you've got a theme installed, your blog is starting to take shape. You now need pages which are just main screens for your site. Almost everyone will need a few basic pages like About Me, Contact and your main Blog page. Beyond that, you might want other pages that are important to your site.

Creating a page is just a matter of clicking on the "Pages" menu item then "Add New." You will give your page a name, add content and images and fill out some SEO information which we will talk about later.

Once all your pages are constructed, you will want to set up your menu which is under the "Appearance" item. Most sites have a Main Menu across the top of their website and a Footer menu that is down at the very bottom. Main menus help people get around while footer menus relay other valuable information like disclaimers and contact info. Place the pages in your menu in the order you want though the About Me page is usually the first on the left.

Next, you'll add plugins to your blog. These are really cool tools that people have created to help you do things without needing to know computer programming. Clicking on "Add New" after "Plugins" will bring up a screen where you can search and select plugins.

Note: Some plugins are free while you'll have to pay for others. I use a few premium plugins but you can build a really great blog on just free ones as well. When looking at new plugins, make sure you look at the most recent update and how many people have downloaded it. Plugins that no one uses might not be updated very often and might stop working.

The plugins I use on my site are:

- Akismet—It comes preloaded on your site and is a great way to protect from spammers in your blog comments. The plugin automatically screens comments and will notify you when a legitimate comment needs approved.

- Broken Link Checker—Nothing is more annoying than clicking on a link in a website and getting a dead end. This plugin monitors all the links on your website and notifies you if one of them is not working.

- Contact Form 7—This is one of the many ways to build contact forms for your site. Easy to use.

- Digg Digg— This is the floating (moving) social share buttons you see on the left-side of the screen. Really a cool way to get people to share your posts.

- EWWW Image Optimizer—Images can slow down the time it takes for your website to load on the computer, which is hugely annoying for visitors. An image optimizer plugin helps to reduce the image file sizes without changing how they look.

- Google XML Sitemaps—This plugin is another must-have because it generates a map of your site to help the search engines (Google, Bing, Yahoo, etc.) to find your blog.

- HelloBar for Wordpress—This is the orange signup bar you see at the top of the screen. Your email subscriber list is absolute gold and you need several ways for collecting emails.

- OptinSkin—This is a paid plugin but offers a nice tool to make pop-ups and subscriber forms. Not an absolute necessity but worth the money since you only need to buy it once and you can use it on as many websites as you want.

- RSS Multi Importer—This puts an RSS feed on your site which can be a nice touch to provide your visitors with content from blogs or news sources you follow. Running a successful blog is all about making for a great visitor experience and giving them the information they need.

- UpPrev—This is a cool feature that pops up a box after a reader has scrolled down a certain distance, say through 70% of the post. The box is customizable and features other posts as kind of a suggestion for further reading.

- WordPress Popular Posts—This plugin displays the most popular posts by comments or views and is customizable for where you want it to show and which posts to show.

- WordPress SEO by Yoast—This is one of the most popular plugins and really helps keep track of your search engine optimization, which we'll get to later.

- WP Polls—This is a handy plugin for making polls for your visitors to answer. It's pretty basic but can help gather some useful information.

- WP Super Cache—This is another one that helps improve your site loading speed.

Most plugins are easy to install and come pre-loaded with the most common settings. You might have to change a few settings to your taste but it's all pretty simple.

Once you've got your plugins installed, you will want to finalize how your site looks by managing widgets. Widgets are just tools that let you place a plugin or item in a certain place on your blog. Go to "Appearance" and then to "Widgets."

Moving these widgets around and customizing them is also pretty easy. You will place them in different spots of your website. The widgets are shown on the left half of the screen and you have website areas on the right side. You just drag a widget to that area and it will show up as a dropdown item (i.e., the Text widget in my Header Right section). By clicking on the dropdown for the widget, you can customize how it shows up on the site.

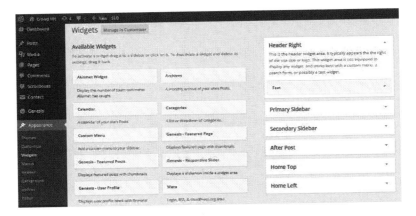

I like to include WordPress Popular Posts and a User Profile at the top of the Primary Sidebar (the right-hand column of the site). That showcases some of your best work for visitors and introduces yourself.

Once your blog is all set up, you will want to start writing. Click on "Posts" and "Add New."

You'll first add the title and the content for the post. I write all my posts up in Microsoft Word and store them in a file for easy organization and then paste it right into WordPress. You can also just type it right into WordPress as well. To link words from your content to another website or to another post in your website, highlight the words and click on the little chain symbol in the tool bar. Input the website address to where you want to link and check the "Open in New Window" box so people clicking the link do not get taken away from your site.

Linking to your other posts helps to keep people reading and helps improve your ranking in Google by telling the search engine that this post is important. Linking to other sites is a helpful way to share information and build relationships with other bloggers.

A note on post length, the standard thinking is that search engines will not look at your post unless it is more than 300 words long. This is misleading and leads to a lot of bloggers pumping out poor quality posts between 400 and 600 words long. Getting found by the search engines is about quality, not quantity. In fact, research on the length of top ten posts that appear in search shows that average length is around 2,000 words.

There are a couple of reasons why this probably happens. First, if you are writing about a specific topic and you cover four pages of material then the post is likely to include a lot of keyword information for the search engines. The other reason is that super-size posts, quality ones anyway, are more likely to have information that is useful to readers. That makes the post more likely to be shared which is a big factor for the search engines. If Google sees that a post is shared hundreds of times then it assumes it must be quality content for the appropriate keywords.

Adding images into your posts is a good way to break up the monotony of reading a long article. Put the cursor where you want the image to show and click "Add Media." You will either add the image from your library or upload it from your computer. You can adjust the size of your images so they do not take up the whole screen. Make sure you include a title, caption and description for the image. The search engines scan images also and it is a way to help your search ranking when someone looks for a keyword.

You will want to add categories to your blog and place your posts in one or more. This helps visitors go directly to material that interests them most. There is a category widget that you can place on your blog that will show the categories and how many posts are in each.

You will also want to add some tags to your post. Tags are a way of telling readers and search engines what the post is about. They are not your keyword but may be variations or other related keywords or phrases. I usually include four tags to every post.

An important part of your post is the Featured Image, selected at the lower-right corner. This is the image that will show on your blog page before people click through to your article. A really interesting image can help persuade people to click through and read the post. As with other images, it is important to add meta information and descriptions so the search engines know what the image is about and can help you get found.

If you installed WordPress SEO by Yoast, making your post search engine friendly is really easy. Search engine optimization (SEO) is a set of tasks that makes your site or individual posts stand out to the search engines like Google and Bing. The more you stand out, the higher up in search you'll appear and the more people will click to your site.

The first part of SEO is picking a keyword that is relevant to the post. A lot of bloggers spend a ton of time picking keywords but I am not really sure it's necessary. Your keyword is the main topic or idea for your post. Having that keyword appear at strategic places in your post, like in image descriptions and your title, will help your article show up in search results when someone types in that word or phrase in Google. Your keyword should be natural to the material and should be pretty easy to pick out after you've written the post. For good keyword optimization:

- Try to have it in the title if it sounds natural

- Try to place the keyword or phrase in the first paragraph or first few sentences

- The "Meta Description" is what will show up to describe the post in search results. It is a one- or two-sentence teaser description and should include the keyword

As mentioned, a lot of people spend tons of time on keywords. They stuff it into the post until reading becomes awkward. They increase the font size of the keyword to the point that it looks ridiculous. These things used to be old tricks to "fool" the search engines but really don't work much anymore. Just write good articles that will interest readers and the search engines will find you.

You can either publish the post immediately by clicking "Publish" or you can schedule it to automatically publish later by clicking "Edit." I write up all my posts at least a few days ahead of schedule and then just load them up. This helps to make sure that you publish new posts regularly even if something comes up at the last minute. Readers appreciate some regularity for a blog and keeping to some kind of a schedule will be rewarded by constant readership.

Blogging Rules to Live By

If you have ever made writing a profession and had to answer to an editor, you will love blogging for the freedom you have over your own material. You still need to proof your posts and make sure it's quality content but you won't have to answer to some kid fresh out of college citing his own personal writing style. That said, there are still some rules you need to follow within the blogoverse.

- **Don't steal!** Copying a post on another website will be discovered. There are plugins that will notify a website if their material is being copied and search engines will punish your website.

- **Don't libel or print false information about someone.** This could open up legal problems and why do you need to bad-mouth someone anyway?

- **Understand fair use of images.** Never use a picture that is copyrighted or that you do not have the right to use. If you are looking for images to use for posts, make sure you are searching within Google for "creative commons," which means that they can be used without permission.

Getting Help with Your Blog

WordPress is extremely easy to use but you still might have times where you just want someone else to set something up. I use freelancers often, mostly for technical stuff where it would take me a while to learn how to do the task. I use two websites, oDesk and Fiverr to find freelancers for projects. It can be frustrating finding qualified people to work on a project because the sites are open to anyone from around the world and they can pretty much write what they like about their credentials. There is a rating system that helps to filter candidates but you will need to spend some time checking experience and even interviewing. For all the time it can take, it is still a good opportunity especially if you find someone that you can just refer to on an ongoing basis.

Step Eight:

DRIVING VISITORS TO YOUR CAMPAIGN BLOG

So you've got a blog for your crowdfunding campaign and you start writing. Then crickets start chirping and you start pulling your hair out because no one is reading it. Believe me, I've been there.

But you're in luck because I am going to share everything I've learned about how to get people to come to your crowdfunding campaign blog. A note though, building a blog that gets regular visitors is not an overnight process even with the best techniques. All the ideas below take time to put together and it will still probably be a couple of months before you see more than a hundred visitors a day.

There are a lot of ways to get people to visit your blog, some legitimate and some not so much. Forget about all the emails you will get that promise to send massive numbers of visitors through directory submissions or blog commenting or whatnot, they don't work and are just a waste of money. Focus your effort on the four methods below and you'll build quality traffic that will be interested in your crowdfunding campaign, not just people from all around the globe that accidentally clicked on a spammed link.

Guest Posting is writing posts for other bloggers to use on their site. What?! It takes long enough to write quality posts; why am I going to just give them away to someone else? Because what is the point of writing posts if no one is there to read them? Other bloggers already have visitors that come by every day. They already have built up their blog's search rankings and get lots of traffic from Google. It is a gift when someone tells you they will host one of your guest posts.

Here is how the process works:

- During the research phase of your crowdfunding pre-launch activities, you are going to be finding other blogs that relate to your crowdfunding campaign. They might be blogs that share the same social cause or cater to people that are interested in a certain product, say tech gadgets.

- Bloggers constantly get emails asking if they will allow a guest post or promote someone's blog. You can't just spam out an email and expect a result. Build up a relationship with these bloggers by reading their blog and posting comments. Ask them for advice on your own blog, your crowdfunding campaign or on your product. Anything to let them know you are out there and a "kindred spirit."

- You don't have to be blood brothers so after a few email exchanges, drop them a line asking to provide a guest post. Propose at least three topics on which you might write about. These should be topics that will interest their readers. Make sure to acknowledge any guest post policies they might have on their site. They might have a certain linking policy you'll have to follow and let them know that you'll respond to any comments left by readers.

- If you don't hear back from someone, send a friendly reminder in a week but don't be pushy. If they answer positively then thank them and make sure you write a strong, informative article. You will want to include one link to your website in the content of the article, preferably to a great post, and another link to your main blog page in a one-paragraph description of your blog.

- You should also provide links to sources of information you referenced but try to limit these to no more than a few.

- I've guest posted on blogs that were scheduled out more than six weeks so you will want to get started on this early if you want to get posts published before your crowdfunding campaign launch.

Guest blogging works on several levels. First, it establishes your name as an expert on a subject and actually reaches an audience. Not everyone that reads your guest post will click through to your blog but a few will make it your way. The more related the blog is to your own blog's subject then the more interested readers are likely to be and the more that will click through.

Guest blogging is also important for your ranking in search engines. Google sees that another blog, maybe a blog that ranks highly for a keyword or topic, provides a link to your website. Google uses this to assume that your blog must be important for that topic as well. Build up enough links to your blog from other quality sites and your own posts will start showing up higher in search rankings. It won't happen overnight but it will happen.

So with guest blogging, you not only get the short-term payoff from a few people clicking through to find your site but also longer-term payoff from more search traffic. It's a great strategy. I try to write at least two guest blog posts for each of my two blogs every month. To get started as a new blog, I would recommend you try doing at least one every week.

Interviews are another important strategy to bring visitors to your site because the person you interview will help bring their own social network. Great interview candidates are either an expert in the subject or have a strong social network or both. Finding these people is going to be a part of your research process but I'll include a few tricks here:

- Search Amazon for books published recently on a given subject. Authors are always looking for a way to promote their book so an interview that talks about the book's subject and links back to the page is a win for everyone.

- Service providers in your crowdfunding campaign's area are another easy target for interviews. You'll need to control the interview to keep it from becoming a commercial. The idea is not to directly promote their product or service but to have them talk about a problem your readers might have and propose a solution. They can include a short paragraph on how their service might help to minimize the problem.

- Other bloggers are good interview candidates as well but they are often busy with their own blog. You might be able to get a short interview from them if you send targeted questions and just ask them to provide one- or two-sentence answers with which you can write up the interview.

- I prefer sending questions through an email and just having the interviewee answer them instead of the traditional phone interview. After you get the answers emailed back, format it for an interview-style post and return it to the interviewee so they can check it over before it goes live on your site. This gives them the opportunity to revise their wording and make sure there are no surprises when it goes on your blog.

- For phone interviews, I use Skype and a handy software program called MP3 Skype Recorder. The software automatically records any conversations you have on Skype and saves the MP3 file on your computer. After the conversation, you can transcribe the interview or have a freelancer do it for you. You'll then need to clean it up and reformat it for a post. Depending on the length, I like to add additional comments to fill out information for readers. You'll then email the drafted interview back to the interviewee to get their feedback and edits.

While interviews posted on your site do not benefit from linking like you get in guest posting, they offer their own benefits. Most obviously, it is your own content on your site and can help with search rankings. The biggest benefit is the introduction of the interviewee's social network. If they are an expert on the topic then they've probably built up a following of people that respect what they say on a certain matter. When the post goes live on your site, send them an email with the link and ask that they share the post with their social network. You may not have much traffic coming to your site but that interviewee could bring massive numbers of visitors through their tweets, Facebook shares and Pinterest pins.

Reaching influencers relates to the prior two methods but is worth its own section because you are going to be asking for something entirely different. Influencers might be journalists, bloggers or even just people that actively post on social media about a certain topic. Just as you link to referenced sources in your blog posts, they provide links to outside sources in their writing.

Those links help your blog in the same way as a guest post does but the difference is that you didn't have to write anything extra. Jackpot.

So how do you find influencers and how do you get them to link to your material?

- Bloggers with highly trafficked sites are a good start. If you download the Alexa toolbar, it will show you the internet ranking of many of the websites you visit. Alexa is an internet ranking and analytics site that gathers visitor information. Blogs or websites with low rankings, lower is better, will make for great links to your site.

- Search for your crowdfunding campaign topic or related topics in Google. Visit the top ten sites and note the author's name and contact information. You might have to search around a bit to find an email address but a Twitter handle is usually easier to find. If you've only got a Twitter name then retweet some of their posts and leave a few comments on their articles for a couple of weeks. Then you can send them a message in Twitter and ask for their email address.

- My favorite way to build a massive influencer list takes some time but is well worth it and you can have some of the work done cheaply by a freelancer.

  O Start out by copying down the top ten results in Google when you search for your topic

  O Go to MOZ Open Site Explorer and paste the URL website address of each result into the search bar. MOZ OSE is another web analytics site like Alexa that provides a ton of information. It is a paid service but the site offers a 30-day free trial, which is all the time you'll need to build your influencer list.

O Putting in the URL website address for each of the top ten in search will show you all the sites that link to that website. Make sure you specify "only external" for Link Source meaning you only want external sites that link in to that post. These are websites or posts, more accurately the authors, which passed the information in that post on to their readers through a link. You will want to filter the results by "DA" which means domain authority and is just a way of measuring the importance of a website. Then copy the first 20 or so URL website addresses of these linking pages. This can all be done in Microsoft Excel by just highlighting the text and copy/paste. I wouldn't try to do it by typing.

O Copying 20 website addresses that link in to each of the top 10 website addresses that show up in a Google search is going to leave you with a list of 200 addresses. Next, you'll do what was noted in the bullet above. Visit each website and find the author's contact email or some other contact information.

O Just as with guest posts, these influencers are not just going to receive an email from a stranger and immediately check out and start linking to your blog. Start the relationship off with a friendly email asking for their advice on something. Mention that you saw their post on topic XYZ and enjoyed the material.

○ Even after building a relationship over a couple of weeks, influencers are not going to automatically start linking to your blog. You still have to create quality information that they will want to pass on to their readers. There are two ways I like to do this. First, super long and detailed posts like this one that provide a ton of information. It is so much easier to give a few excerpts and link to a 20-page source than it is to recreate all that information. The other excellent way for getting links is through infographics. Interesting graphics that tell a story take a little longer to create, though you can find help on Fiverr that will do the design work, but they are well worth it when it comes to attracting links. There are websites that will generate a code that you can put under your infographic so others can feature the image on their website and a link is automatically created.

○ Only when you have some truly great content that is worthy of a link, reach out to your influencer list through an email. Tell them you respect their expertise on the subject and wanted to get their feedback on a recent post or infographic you created. Not everyone will check it out or respond but even a 15% response rate means 30 people from your list of 200. Some will share immediately through social share buttons on your website and some may even provide a link back to your material in a

future post of their own.

Social media is actually a surprisingly small portion of the visitor traffic to most established blogs but is a bigger help for new sites. Numbers vary but most of the established blogs I follow only get about 20% or less of their total traffic from social media and often about half of that is from one site . . . and it's not Facebook. Still, with your new crowdfunding campaign blog you are probably not getting much of any traffic from search engines for at least a couple of months. Visitors from guest posts, interviews and influencers will start to trickle in but those take time as well. Social media posts offer the opportunity to get at least a few people to read your blog and it is pretty easy to post and participate on the sites.

Some people spend a lot of time on social media but you'll want to focus your crowdfunding campaign blog on four sites: Facebook, Twitter, LinkedIn and Pinterest.

- Do I even need to talk about **Facebook**? With more than 1.3 billion visitors, the site is pretty much obligatory for everyone. You should have a Facebook page for your crowdfunding campaign and a personal page for yourself. Pasting the URL website address of your blog posts into the updates box on the Facebook page will generate a link and image from the post. Make sure to add a little detail by writing something else about the post. You will want to share the post on your own personal page and within relevant groups but don't just spam it out everywhere. Social media is about providing relevant information that benefits the reader.

- Don't make the common mistake and think that your entire social media strategy is simply reposting your blog posts on the social networks. Social media is a two-way street; otherwise, it wouldn't be *social*. Sharing other people's posts will help put you on their radar for a guest post or link in the future and will provide valuable content to your followers. You'll also want to ask and answer questions to build that truly social relationship.

- **Twitter** is another social network, but your posts are limited to 140 characters. These tweets can be everything from updating followers on what you're doing or how you're feeling to tweeting out a link to your recent blog post. I tweet out my new blog posts four times on the day they are published. This is because the sheer volume of tweets most people get means that yours is quickly buried unless someone is glued to their Twitter feed. With tweets, you will need to include the image manually because it won't automatically generate from the pasted URL address. You'll want to include the post's image in at least one tweet because posts with images are much more likely to be shared and clicked.

- Again, you will want to share other people's tweets as a way of providing that social experience and quality stream of information to your community. Applications like the Buffer App make all this so much easier. Buffer will link up with your social media accounts and allow you to schedule tweets and retweets. The free version allows you to schedule up to 10 tweets at a time. This means you can keep a fairly constant flow of information going out to followers without having to constantly visit Twitter to send something out.

- **LinkedIn** is like Facebook for professionals. You may not necessarily need a profile on the site but it can send some good traffic to your crowdfunding campaign blog. The important thing to remember with LinkedIn is to keep it professional. You are not going to be posting pictures of your cat in the sweater you knitted. Look for groups on the site that might be interested in the topic related to your crowdfunding campaign. There are also a few crowdfunding groups where you can ask for advice and reach out to others.

- I avoided **Pinterest** for a long time until I realized that it accounts for the majority of social media traffic to a lot of blogs. Pinterest is a social media site where people "pin" images and provide descriptions and links to the post related to the image. I always thought of Pinterest as only applicable to blogs or websites that had a visual appeal like a blog on art. Boy was I wrong! One personal finance blogger I know gets around 1,000 visitors to her blog every day just from her Pinterest profile, way more than she gets from the 4,600 people that have "Liked" her Facebook page.

- On your Pinterest page, you create "boards" which are areas where you pin images related to a specific topic. People surf Pinterest looking for interesting images and content and will click through your pins to read the related information. It is important to keep your boards and the pins you put in them specific. Visitors can follow your profile or just one of your boards and will get a notification when you pin something new.

Notice I didn't include **Search** as one of the ways to drive traffic to your crowdfunding blog, despite the fact that traffic from search engines accounts for more than a third of my own traffic. It's because I don't think search rankings can be "gamed" like so many would have you believe. Write good quality material for your blog that focuses on a specific topic and that readers will find useful.

Step Nine:

Turning Blog Visitors into Campaign Success

After two chapters of reading how to create and draw people to your crowdfunding blog, you'll be happy to hear that turning your blog's followers into crowdfunding campaign support is a pretty easy process.

You've already proven yourself an expert on your campaign topic and put in the time to convince people that you're serious about your crowdfunding project.

Following the steps in the prior chapters, you will have brought thousands to your crowdfunding blog over a few months. The numbers are going to work in your favor. Over 1.4 million pledges, the average pledge support is $71 on Kickstarter. Over three months of blogging, you should be able to draw at least 4,500 visitors. If even 3% of those visitors become financial supporters of your crowdfunding campaign you will have reached 135 backers and nearly $10,000 for your campaign, all just from blogging!

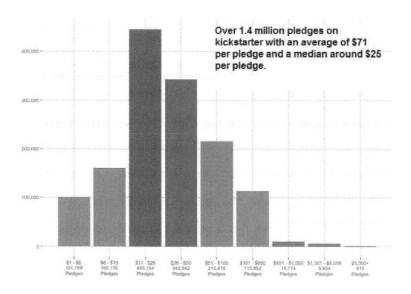

Over 1.4 million pledges on kickstarter with an average of $71 per pledge and a median around $25 per pledge.

But those people are not going to be jumping to your crowdfunding campaign to pledge their support without any work on your part.

Throw a Launch Party

Probably the most fun you'll have with your crowdfunding campaign is the launch party. Even if your crowdfunding campaign isn't local in nature, getting 50 people together to talk about the campaign and get excited about the launch can give it a life of its own.

Leading up to the launch, but at least a month in advance, start talking to email subscribers about the idea of a launch party. This should give you an idea about how many might be interested. You'll want to talk to some of your most passionate supporters about helping out with the party, maybe reaching out to their high-profile contacts or friends in the press.

You don't have to go Kardashian with the budget. If you can bring in a large group of people, you shouldn't have too hard a time partnering with a local establishment. One crowdfunding campaign hosted their launch party at a local bar with the campaign owners serving as bartenders for a few hours during the night. In exchange for the crowd, the bar helped pay for marketing the event and discounted drinks.

It helps to have at least two or three people that can act as firestarters at the launch, people that share your passion for the campaign and are not shy about spreading their excitement. You and your team of fire-starters should meet up before the party to put together talking points and ideas.

Besides building excitement, you need to work out how you are going to ask for financial support. According to the Public Management Institute, not asking is the single biggest mistake in fundraising. Only 56% of households say they have been asked to give to at least one non-profit but 95% of these say they gave to at least one. People will donate if they are asked, especially if they've come to your launch party in support.

Your goal is going to be to raise 20% of your crowdfunding campaign goal at the launch party. Take a page from non-profits and set up a movable board to track your progress. Backers do not have to offer a live donation at the event but can write a pledge card and go to the campaign page later. Raising 20% at the launch party will put you well on your way to success. Data shows that crowdfunding campaigns that reach 30% of their campaign goal have a 90% chance of being fully funded.

Of course, you'll want to reach out to your blog email subscribers that are not able to attend the launch party for a contribution as well. Tell them you were disappointed that they could not make it but understand and appreciate their support.

How to Ask for the Pledge

Whole books have been written on fundraising and salesmanship. Your own process can be pretty detailed but I am going to run down a few points that have always worked for me.

- Start the conversation off talking about how excited you are to get the campaign started and how much the crowdfunding campaign means to not just yourself but a wider community.

- Don't spend more than a few minutes building up to the request. If you've already built a personal relationship with your subscribers and contacts, they shouldn't need much build-up.

- In asking for a pledge, be confident and don't be afraid to ask for a higher amount. You already know that they are interested in your campaign, you just don't know exactly how interested. Start with the highest level of reward offered for your campaign. You won't get it unless you ask.

- If they are reluctant initially, have another brief pitch that will reinforce the key points and emotional need for the campaign. Then ask for a pledge at another reward level. Don't forget to emphasize what they get and what need the campaign will be able to fulfill with their contribution.

- If they are still not willing to pledge a contribution, try asking for one of the lowest reward levels. Emphasize that it really isn't the money at these levels but the ability to show backer support for that social proof that is important on the internet.

In my experience, there is no such thing as a natural salesperson. Whether through formal on-the-job training or just life experiences, people learn how to approach others and share their passion for a product or cause. If you haven't got this experience or the time to learn salesmanship, prior planning will go a long way. Think through the sales process from building the relationship to the request. Practice your pitch with friends, family and active supporters. Learn what the most common rejection excuses are and practice rebuttals that will turn reluctance into support.

Email Subscribers are Pure Gold

Turning crowdfunding blog visitors into supporters is where your email list really comes into play. Subscribers should receive an introductory email after they sign up but your goal should be a personal call within a week. Even with social media, the web can be a really impersonal place. Building a personal connection with each subscriber will help build a sense of community.

Your email list will also help gauge each subscriber's level of commitment. Through mail services like MailChimp, you'll be able to see who opens your regular newsletters and clicks through any links in emails. People that regularly open and click on links may be good candidates for a bigger role in the campaign.

Some bloggers send out daily or twice-weekly emails to their subscribers. I send out a weekly newsletter for both of my blogs. You'll have to decide how often to send out emails or newsletters. I wouldn't send them out daily unless you've got an extremely passionate following and post to your blog nearly every day. You may want to increase the frequency of emails leading up to the campaign launch. Build a sense of urgency with a series of emails, something like a countdown to the campaign. You'll be able to carry that momentum through to your campaign.

Blog Visitors are More than Just Dollar Signs

This really goes for all of your supporters and is one of the most overlooked ways to boost your crowdfunding campaign. First, you need to know your supporters and subscribers personally. You should aim to do this as a way to make the campaign personal anyway but it will also give you a chance to understand how to use their strengths for more than financial support.

Some of your supporters may be natural marketers or good business planners. Do any of them have experience in video or photography production? Can they write for your blog or post on another blog? Do they have any media or internet contacts that might help the campaign go viral?

Even getting your supporters to pass your crowdfunding campaign page or blog through their social network can help bring hundreds of new people to the cause. You have to ask though and you might have to ask a couple of times. There's no room for the shy in crowdfunding.

Reworking your Crowdfunding Blog after Campaign Launch

Once your crowdfunding campaign is live, you will need to put in some time to put in links and promote your campaign on the blog. Every page and post should have a short paragraph about your campaign and a link to the page. The paragraph can be pretty easily written in to each page. It helps to have an image that is clickable to your campaign as well.

For posts, there are a couple different ways you can do it. If you have only been posting once or twice per week, you may not have more than 30 or so posts. You can go through each one manually and input the paragraph. If you would rather save a little time, you can automatically put linkable text through a plugin like Optin Skin or Optin Monster at a certain spot or at the end of every post.

You will also want to put a clickable image, or banner ad, in the header of your website that will appear on every page. You won't get massive amounts of visitors from these links and ads but every pledge counts.

Blogging for Crowdfunding Campaigns: Wrapping Up

Running your crowdfunding campaign blog successfully will take time but it will be well worth it in terms of meeting your campaign goal. Before you let the blog go dark after the campaign, consider keeping it going with a few posts every month. In less than a year, you will see the site's search rankings increase significantly and the traffic you get from Google alone may be able to power your next crowdfunding campaign.

Step Ten:

MARKETING: BUILDING PRE-LAUNCH ENTHUSIASM

While you can do all your crowdfunding campaign marketing with almost no budget at all, should you?

Even established multi-national charities have to spend money on expenses and marketing. The American Red Cross is one of the most efficient organizations but still spends about 8% of its total contributions on expenses. Other charities spend much more but the average seems to be around 15% of contributions to expenses.

For small business, spending on marketing is a given and built into budgets from day one. In fact, marketing is one of the largest expenses for most new businesses.

Building marketing and other expenses into your campaign budget will go a long way to establishing credibility with supporters. No one expects you to do everything for free and it wouldn't be realistic to think you could. Working through how much everything will cost will show supporters that you have taken the time and are serious about the cause.

Budgeting crowdfunding campaign marketing does not mean you have to blow thousands to convert people into backers. Most crowdfunding campaign marketing can be done for free and you can build a huge community if you give it a few months. If you don't have a few months to build your crowdfunding community, use some of the resources below to get the best bang for your buck.

Crowdfunding Marketing Resources for your Campaign

The marketing resources and sites below do not include project fees or fulfillment costs for your campaign. Those mandatory costs need to come out of your budget before deciding how much you can spend on marketing services or applications.

Service providers can be hired to manage all the resources below or you can manage them yourself. There are a few important things to remember here.

- Building a true community will take at least a couple of months and trying to rush it through expensive third-party providers will not necessarily pay off in more backers.

- Your time is valuable. It may be more cost effective to hire out an expert to manage one or more resources than having to learn and do everything yourself.

- We all have our favorite web hangouts and sites so it's best to spread your advertising budget around to several areas rather than focus on one specific website or resource. The starter package for advertising through most resources includes most of the benefit you'll need and will reach your most targeted audience. Resist the urge to buy into larger and more complicated offers even if they only cost a few dollars more.

Social Media

Facebook is the Holy Grail of social media. With more than a billion users globally, the site is seemingly universal in some social circles. Unfortunately, you won't be the first to push your campaign through the site and people have grown immune to many requests for support. Rather than run your crowdfunding campaign through your personal profile, set up a separate page to focus and build community. You'll still want to share all the updates through your personal network but your campaign page will help you target your community building around the campaign.

Facebook offers advertising to promote your page and specific posts and the ability to target your advertising to specific groups and geographic areas like the United States. Be warned though that there is a whole industry built up around clicking on advertisements to collect commissions and the "likes" you receive through these campaigns may not actually translate to real action. In fact, these fake likes may actually hurt your outreach on Facebook. The site only sends out your updates to a sample of your followers. If those followers click on your update, Facebook figures the update is newsworthy and sends it out to more of your network. Those artificially generated likes are less likely to click on updates which may stop those updates from being sent out to more of your network.

- Through your campaign's page, you can schedule posts for different times of the day. Take advantage of this feature to constantly connect with followers

- Like all social media networks, real community starts with a personal plea. Spamming out a request to all your friends to join your Facebook page will usually be met with disappointing results. Reach out at least with a personal email or preferably with a phone call to your contacts asking them to join your page and regularly share posts.

If you're crowdfunding campaign or product is business-related, **LinkedIn** may be just as important to your efforts as Facebook. There are more than 300 million users on the business networking site and I've found the groups much easier to use than those on Facebook. The site offers subscription services that allow you greater access to search and messaging. Use the free month offer to try out the site but the free membership is all I have ever really needed.

- Make sure to reach out to colleagues for a testimonial on your profile to build social proof in your abilities.

- Detail your profile with as much information as is relevant and include a professional picture.

- Even if your crowdfunding campaign is not business related, LinkedIn can help to connect with influencers in different industries

Twitter is probably the most recognized social media tool after Facebook and an easy one to use for your crowdfunding campaign marketing. The site is limited because your tweets can only be up to 140 characters but you'll be surprised at how much traction you can get from each post.

- Download the **Buffer** app to schedule up to 10 tweets throughout the day.

- Research the number of searches for different hashtags relevant to your campaign through sites like hashtags.org and include one hashtag in each tweet.

- Create a list of influencers in your industry and their Twitter @ name. Calling out to influencers or news retweeting users within your tweets will help increase your reach.

- Don't just tweet out your own posts. Keep a regular schedule of your own updates and relevant or interesting tweets from others to help build community.

Video Production and Editing

Your crowdfunding campaign marketing video is one of the few places I would say you will definitely want to spend a little money. Unless you have the video equipment and experience, it is usually cheaper to hire out some for these services than to do it all yourself. That doesn't mean you have to spend thousands on a series of quality videos but a budget of a few hundred will go a long way.

- Produce a series of short videos at once instead of having to hire services for multiple shoots. You will use your intro video for your main campaign page but the other videos can be uploaded to YouTube for super-charged viral marketing.

- Put just as much thought into pre-production writing and rehearsal as you can to save time and money during the video shoot.

- If your campaign is focused on the local market, include local backdrops and influencers in your videos.

- The Fundrazr blog offers some more detail on video production from pre-production through the editing process.

Online Advertising

Online advertising includes a range of resources but can get really expensive. I have found the best success in Google AdWords and press releases. Before you blanket the internet with ads, spend some time thinking about who you really want to come to your website or crowdfunding campaign. Resist the urge to buy keyword advertising for high-volume traffic that may not really be interested in your cause.

- Focus on a couple of keywords and set a really small budget first to see how well the advertising leads to traffic and support on your campaign. Make use of the geographic targeting available on the advertising platforms

- Press releases can be cost effective and go out to a wide audience but you need to be more strategic than simply spamming out your release. Develop a rapport with key journalists by reading their articles and responding before your release. If they know you by name, they are more likely to recognize your press release when it comes out.

- Content is king and can be the most effective online advertising but can also take months to build an audience. If you have the time (i.e., several months before your campaign launch, set up a blog and start writing about the cause around your campaign. This will help set you up as an expert in the field and build your community.

Online Forums

Forums on websites related to your cause or company may actually fit under social media but the idea is so important and often overlooked that I wanted to call it out separately. Find two or three forums that relate to your campaign and spend a couple of months contributing and getting to know the most active contributors.

- Active forum contributors will be your most enthusiastic supporters because they are already interested in the cause.

- Spending time on forums will help learn the biggest issues and questions people have in your cause or industry

Offline advertising may be the most cost-effective resource if your cause or business is local in nature. Online social networks have grown so crowded and impersonal in some ways that it is getting increasingly easy to ignore the advertising. Reaching out to people on a face-to-face level may be harder than a few mouse clicks but you'll build community for your campaign much faster.

The biggest shock for most campaigns is the amount of time it takes to build community and support the **ongoing interactions with backers**. Regular interactions, online and on a personal-level, are the most important facets of a campaign. Taking more than a day to respond to an email or not reaching out regularly risks losing any momentum you've built in other marketing resources.

- This is another one of the areas where I recommend spending a little money but you need to find someone that is just as passionate about the cause. Instead of hiring out a part-time worker, you might try reaching out to current supporters with a small weekly stipend to help out.

- Build your community through a couple of your most enthusiastic supporters, preferably pre-launch, to get them onboard with a few hours of outreach support each week. In the first week, each of you should focus on a few of the more enthusiastic supporters that will also commit a little time. With this team of outreach specialists, you can start focusing on reaching out for financial support.

The Best Bang for Your Crowdfunding Buck

A lot of crowdfunding success comes down to the time you are willing and able to spend on the campaign. Planning your resources and campaign at least two to three months ahead of the official launch can save you a ton of money because it allows you time to build community within the free resources instead of having to speed up your marketing through paid services.

Within my own experience with marketing resources, I've found pretty good results through conservative budgets on the social networks and Google AdWords. If you start a blog or website for your campaign, something to definitely consider if it's going to be an ongoing business or cause, then you'll usually get a few hundred dollars worth of free advertising credits when you pay for your website.

The idea is not to build a huge following through advertising but to just draw a few targeted people to the website or campaign. It is through this first group of supporters that you will work through to reach others but you'll be able to do it with your community than with advertising dollars.

Breaking your crowdfunding campaign into several smaller campaigns will help you test crowdfunding marketing resources on a smaller scale first. Plan on raising seed funding for your cause or idea first, and budget a small amount to the most essential marketing resources. You are more likely to be able to hit your target for smaller campaigns and you can use the marketing information in your subsequent campaigns.

Even with pledges to crowdfunding campaigns nearly doubling every year, most campaigns are disappointed to find that there really is no crowd in crowdfunding. Without a crowdfunding marketing strategy, you are likely to join the 60% of campaigns that fail to reach their funding goal.

Step Eleven:

PRE-LAUNCH CROWDFUNDING HACKS

We've walked through most of the steps in your pre-launch crowdfunding campaign but there are still a few odds and ends that will help you get to fully funded. Some of these apply to research, outreach or another area while some really defy categorization. I've included them here because they deserve special attention.

Making Connections

Pre-launch crowdfunding is a lot like playing the game, Six Degrees of Kevin Bacon. If you have never played it, the idea is that any two people on earth can be connected by six or fewer acquaintances. In the game, you try to match up any random actor or actress with Kevin Bacon by people they have worked with in films.

In crowdfunding, your best connections are going to be those that start with your established personal network. Thinking through your existing personal network can help uncover opportunities to connect with influencers or journalists.

Getting people onboard with your project early is not only about funding but also provides a lot of social proof to other potential backers. The internet is still a very uncertain and untrusted place for a lot of people. Seeing that you already have a lot of people that believe in you and your project will go a long way in establishing trust.

Building a List

Run a Contest –This is a common strategy and can be affective but there is a caveat. You want to offer something that attracts a large audience and is valuable but try to make it something related to your business or cause. Attracting a thousand people that will ultimately have no interest in your crowdfunding campaign may not be worth your time.

Build a Free Plugin – Free applications or plugins are a great incentive for people to sign up to your email list or register on your website. There are a few websites that make it fairly easy and you don't have to be a tech guru. Check out ibuildapp.com for their free service.

Include an Email Signup Link in your Signature - In crowdfunding, your email list is money in the bank. Make it easy for people to follow you by posting a link to your email list signup form everywhere. There are several email list sites on the web but MailChimp and Aweber are the most popular. You can use MailChimp for free up to 2,000 subscribers which is likely all you'll need.

Don't Forget to Ask

Before you are ready to launch your crowdfunding campaign, fundraise from your community for at least three weeks. Actively reach out to your network and ask for their financial support and with a simple task. This gives them an option and you will likely get some volunteer work rather than a straight no answer.

Try offering people the opportunity for conditional support. Their financial promise only kicks in if you raise a certain percentage, say 20% or 30% of your goal. This lets them know that you are committed to making the campaign a success and will work hard to get there. You'll get through a lot of no responses with this strategy.

I would not start a crowdfunding campaign unless I had at least 15% of my funding goal pre-committed through pre-launch crowdfunding. Data shows that campaigns that start with no funding have just a 15% chance at reaching their goal while those with 5% pre-funded have a 50% chance at meeting their goal. Beyond the data, if the crowdfunding platform sees your campaign doing well, it might just consider placing you on the front page as a featured project.

RUNNING A SUCCESSFUL CROWDFUNDING CAMPAIGN

After months of planning and preparation, you are finally ready to actually start crowdfunding! If you have followed the pre-launch steps closely, the month or two when you crowdfunding campaign is live could be relatively easy. You will still have to work to keep your community motivated but good pre-launch momentum can help take a lot of the burden off of your shoulders.

Step Twelve:

STARTING YOUR CAMPAIGN THE RIGHT WAY

So you've spent months pre-launching your crowdfunding campaign, creating your outreach list and building a community around the campaign. You have a strong team around the project that is just as passionate about it as you are and you've ironed out all the wrinkles in the idea.

Now what?

Now you're actually ready to start crowdfunding! You are ready to put your campaign down on a platform and launch the project.

Making your Crowdfunding Idea a Crowdfunding Campaign

The actual pieces of your campaign page will be slightly different depending on which platform you choose. I will describe the process for a Kickstarter page below but most of the ideas will be generalizable across any platform. Opening an account on any of the sites is pretty easy, just putting in some personal information and choosing your screen name.

While the campaign title should be something catchy and interesting, you want to use your real name as the creator of the project. For the creator's image, choose a picture of yourself that will show up clearly in a very small size. This is so your friends and family will easily recognize the campaign as yours when they visit the page.

Shorter campaigns create more sense of urgency while longer campaigns give you more time to raise money. Generally, campaigns of 30 to 45 days work best and should be all you need if you've already put in the time pre-launching the idea. Most campaigns start and end strong but fizzle out during the middle period. This can lead to terrific disappointment and cause you to lose faith and motivation. It's best to set a shorter campaign to minimize the cursed mid-campaign period and keep a greater sense of urgency on backers.

*Make sure you plan your crowdfunding schedule so that your campaign does not end on a holiday or a weekend. Most campaigns see their best support over the last few days. It's best to have people around their computers to see your outreach and marketing. It will likely take the platform staff a couple of days to approve the campaign so plan accordingly.

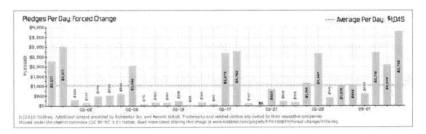

Pro tip: Schedule your campaign around an industry conference or some kind of convention of people that might be interested in your product. Having a demo model on hand to show people can be a great way to get over the uncertainty of the internet. Nearly everyone has a tablet or smartphone now and can go directly to your campaign page after talking with you.

Parts of the Crowdfunding Page

Your first decision will be one of the most critical, what should you call your crowdfunding campaign? It may seem superficial and a little unfair but your page title is going to be a big factor in getting people to your campaign. When asked why the clicked on a specific post, six out of ten participants in an internet study claimed title as their top reason.

While you want your campaign title to be relevant to the product, there's nothing wrong with spicing it up a little. Most campaigns use their product name followed by a colon (:) and then some kind of interesting descriptive. You might try your slogan if it is interesting or descriptive enough to grab someone's attention. Spend a little time brainstorming at least three or four titles and then run them by someone on the team.

Next, choose around ten images that really show the product from a visual perspective. These images should speak to the need your product satisfies for customers or fans. The best image will be your cover and the rest will be used throughout the campaign page.

I use Rennik Soholt's Forced Change campaign a lot here in the guide because it was such a well-crafted campaign. For the campaign page, Rennik used pictures that showed the horrible aftermath of Hurricane Katrina and Rita and other pictures of the people in his documentary. After seeing the devastation on the region, you really get a feeling for the cause by seeing images of the people that lived through it.

Immediately following your video on the page should be your 30-second elevator pitch. Written down, this will probably be about two short paragraphs. For many people that visit your page, this may be as far down as they read and it's your only chance to convert casual internet surfers to backers.

Your pitch needs four elements:

- It needs to be relatable—Only people that can put themselves in the shoes of your cause's beneficiaries or that can see themselves using your product are going to support it. Make your pitch generalizable enough that people associate with it.

- Urgency—People need to understand why they should care and why your campaign needs supported NOW! Build in milestone deadlines, preferential terms on contracts, anything to create that sense of urgency.

- It needs to leave them wanting more—You need to set up a problem and hint at how your product or cause can solve it but don't try to fit the solution into your short pitch. Few will have the patience to read through a complete case here in the first few paragraphs. Even if you are able to squeeze in that much info in a few short sentences, if you've answered all the questions then there's no reason to read further. At this point, people probably haven't spent enough time looking around to be converted to backers. You want them saying, "Okay, sounds interesting. What else do we have here?" After spending some time on the page, visitors are much more likely to have enough buy-in to become a backer.

- The ask! Don't forget to actually tell people how they can make a difference and ask for them to join the community around your campaign. Don't just ask people to become backers, ask them to reach out to you and be a part of the team.

If your elevator pitch did its job then people are primed to read a longer description of your crowdfunding campaign.

Consider a strong image after the pitch and then lead into the full description of your campaign.

Elements that work within a larger campaign description:

- That same sense of urgency you were building in your pitch will work here as well.

- Offer the opportunity for people to be a part of something bigger than themselves. This is one of the defining characteristics of crowdfunding, people feel like they are a part of the product or cause. By becoming backers, people feel like they have helped you achieve something otherwise unattainable.

- Being able to get something before it is publicly available is a strong draw for many. Build exclusivity and trendiness into your campaign for its backers.

Be honest and conversational in your campaign page. Crowdfunding is first and foremost a social tool and people want to be reached on a personal level. Talking in the first person, using pronouns like I, you and me will help make this connection.

Include links to your website in the bio and link all your social network sites into the campaign page. Don't forget to ask people to click through and be a part of the community on your Twitter, Facebook and your other social network profiles. Don't assume that people are on the same social platforms as you. Make it easy for people to join the community from whichever social platform they prefer.

You should itemize your budget but keep it conversational. Talk about how much it will cost for major budget items and how important they are for the project. Listing out your budget and talking through it will help build credibility and prove that you've thought the project through completely. Visitors will appreciate that you are being upfront with how their money will be used.

Finally, you will want to talk through a realistic timeline for the campaign. Include a brief summary of everything you did during the pre-launch of the campaign to show people just how hard you've worked on the project.

Describe a few what-if scenarios for reward fulfillment and project completion. Knowing that reward promises will be fulfilled is one of the biggest uncertainties in crowdfunding, unfortunately because many campaigns fail to come through and deliver. Being honest and talking about different scenarios will solve a lot of problems before they occur and will help build credibility.

I generally recommend to people that they take their estimated number of days to complete production and rewards fulfillment and then add another 20% on top for the timeline. People are almost universally optimistic in their planning and it is best to deliver earlier rather than later than what people expect, especially if you ever want to crowdfund again.

Once you've got your campaign page written out, let it set for at least a day. Have one or two other people look it over and provide feedback. If you submit your campaign for review immediately after having written it up, you are much less likely to catch any mistakes. After you've let it sit for a day and gotten feedback from others on the team, read through it and see if there's room for improvement.

After submitting your page for review to the crowdfunding platform staff, you'll need to review it again and agree to the platform's terms before it goes live.

Your Crowdfunding Clock is Ticking!

Now the pressure is on. Your crowdfunding campaign is live. You've got a date and a funding goal to reach. Your community of backers should be just as enthusiastic as you are for the campaign to start so make sure you reach out and give them a link to the campaign page. It is extremely important that you emphasize the need for pledges on the first day. Campaigns that can meet 20% or more of their funding goal on the first day have a better chance of being featured on most platforms.

If you haven't already, you need to have a day-by-day marketing and planning schedule for your crowdfunding campaign. You've only got a few weeks and you need to use every day to its fullest. You do not need to reach out on every social network or through every channel on a daily basis but you do need to hit each one at least every week. It's also a good idea to schedule in a few campaign updates so you can show page visitors that you are still attentive to the campaign. Make sure you know how you are going to get from your campaign start to campaign finish and success before you get there.

Step Thirteen:

MAKE IT PERSONAL AND MAKE AN IMPACT

Crowdfunding has the potential to open up the world of start-up financing to millions and fund crowdfunding campaigns around the world. Crowdfunding in 2012 reached $2.7 billion, an 81% increase from the prior year and grew to over $5.0 billion in 2013.

Just a year after passage of Title II of the JOBS Act saw a total of 534 companies successfully meet their crowdfunding campaign goal for equity participation. More than $200 million in equity capital was raised, averaging a little over $400k per company and when Title III of the JOBS Act opens the door to investment to everyone, the market could boom higher.

But despite the huge growth in crowdfunding, nearly 60% of creative campaigns and more than 80% of equity campaigns miss their funding goal. Why is it that more than half of crowdfunding campaigns fail to reach their target?

Because the people running the crowdfunding campaigns are using the same rules they learned in marketing 101 instead of following crowdfunding concepts. Crowdfunding is not traditional fundraising and you cannot follow traditional marketing concepts.

Tap your Social Animal

Despite the rise of social media and interconnectedness today, the internet still feels like a very impersonal experience for many people. Anonymous comments are used as a way to rant on once taboo subjects and social connections developed on sites like Facebook only rarely lead to any type of interaction.

But we are social creatures and we crave interaction with other people. Why do you suppose reality TV has become so popular, besides as a means of feeling good about your own lot in life? Because people want to feel involved in the lives of others. They want to share life experiences and be a part of a community. The sad fact is that most of us do not have much an opportunity to feel that sense of community within our hectic schedules.

Up until the crowdfunding revolution, most people's exposure to marketing has been through commercials that have gotten so inane that we have learned to unconsciously block them out.

Put it together and you have a huge opportunity for your crowdfunding campaign. An opportunity that, sadly, goes untapped by most projects. There are 6,558 of projects seeking funding on Kickstarter and 15,974 companies on Crowdfunder right now. Data shows that most will not get funded.

Why?

Because it's business, not personal. Projects, especially those seeking equity funding, focus so much on the numbers and the straight-forward business pitch that they forget the power of personality.

Forget what you thought you knew about the world of finance. **In crowdfunding; it's personal, not business.**

You need to form an immediate bond with anyone reading your project description. In our world of fast-food and faster YouTube clips, you have very little time to reach someone before they decide to click to the next project. Pick out a couple of sentences about your project that evoke the most emotion and describe the project in results. These points should go to the top of your description before anything else and preferably in bullet points.

Ultimately, many people will want to donate or invest in your project simply because they want to be a part of your journey. That is why you need to tell your story, how you got to this point and how the project is the natural path through that story.

Relating your project as a story and making it a personal journey will go a long way to making an impact on others.

Participation is essential in your project and could be the difference between getting funded or not. Give people a good story and they will likely help out with a donation. Give them a chance to be part of something bigger than themselves and they will be busting your door down to help.

- Find ways to make your project personal.
    - Tell your story.
    - Find ways that make your story and your project relatable to others.
    - Highlight the emotions evoked in your story and your campaign.
    - Tell people what their involvement means and how they can be more than just a donation.

Evoke Emotions through Sight and Sound

Most campaigns fall far short when it comes to appealing to our senses. Understand that people have probably read through a dozen or more campaigns before getting to yours. Believe me, the reading gets old after a while.

Use graphic images, video and audio files throughout your project request. For images, hire a professional photographer to take some shots directly related to your location or cause if it's applicable. You can also source images on websites like Flickr and Google but you need to make sure they are free of copyright issues.

Finding images on Flickr:

- Go to the website and click "Explore."

- Click "The Commons" for pictures that can be used in the public domain

- Search for your keywords or pictures you want to find

Finding images on Google:

- Go to Google Images and search for a keyword

- Click "Search Tools" then "Usage Rights"

- You will want to filter for those that can be reused with or without modification depending on what you plan on doing with them

If you are posting a video, you should be in it. Few of us consider ourselves incredibly photogenic and you need to get over any fear you have of public speaking. A crowdfunding campaign is as much about selling yourself and your story as it is about selling your project. Here again, it's good to hire someone with their own equipment and experience to manage your video creation. Even with the extra cost, you'll probably save money by not having to buy the equipment or spend time figuring out editing software.

Yancey Strickler, cofounder of Kickstarter, reports that projects with videos have had a success rate of 54% while those without a video have only been successfully funded 39% of the time. We are sensory creatures and any way you can draw upon all five senses will help. Make a video of your project, even if it is just a brief one-minute teaser to the bigger project request.

Simple audio files of testimonials and your own appeals to supporters can really drive a campaign if strategically positioned around your campaign page. Beyond your own campaign page, these additional media items can be used around the web to bring attention to your project. Post videos on YouTube and your images on Flickr for extra reach.

- Reach out to supporters through images, video and audio to really distinguish your project,

- Videos are a must and you should be in it, if only for a brief teaser video to drive home the important points of your campaign.

- Make sure you use images that evoke emotion and are free of copyright license.

- Use your videos, images and audio files around the web to reach more people and integrate the social experience.

Taking it beyond Friends and Family

As with most of the ideas here, participation starts with your own close network of friends and family. Consider hosting a dinner to highlight your project. Give a presentation, including your video and talk to everyone about the project. Chances are, if you cannot draw your closest circle into the project with your vision and passion, you will probably have a hard time doing it with total strangers.

Event planning tips:

- Write out your goals for the event. How much money do you want to raise? How many people do you want to sign up to help out?

- Make sure your event does not conflict with a holiday or another important event.

- Talk to people or organizations early to line up sponsorship donations to help fund your event.

- If it's a public event, talk to the local newspapers and television to get the word out.

- Build interest through Facebook, Google Hangouts, and Twitter a week or two before the event.

- Get local bloggers involved by writing a guest post on their site.

- Have a backup plan for weather or if any service providers fail to come through.

Once you've started registering interest in the campaign, every donor or investor needs to be contacted to ask what they do and to be interviewed on what they can bring to the project. That initial monetary commitment means they relate to your message and believe in what you're doing. Use that association to build a relationship and drive other forms of help.

Supporters may be able to provide services within their profession or connect you to someone they know that offers services you need. They may be active in social groups and can offer an introduction. Interviewing new donors or investors will open up a lot of information on the effectiveness of your ask and may just find someone as passionate about the project as you are.

- Host a dinner or event with friends and family to talk about the project.

- Expand your event, or hold another, for the general public.

- Reach out personally to supporters and help them find ways to be involved in the project.

Making your campaign personal will go a long way in drawing people to the idea and even making them more than just monetary contributors. Anyone that has run a crowdfunding campaign can tell you it is an immense amount of work and the non-monetary help you get from supporters is just as valuable as the donations. Remember to use different forms of media in your campaign and use special events to closely connect with your biggest supporters.

Step Fourteen:

BUILDING COMMUNITY AROUND YOUR CAMPAIGN

The explosion in crowdfunding, especially for rewards-based projects, over the last several years has made people think that raising money is as simple as posting a project on one of the popular sites. A couple of days are spent putting together a proposal and a brief budget. The project is posted and the entrepreneur waits for the money to roll in.

And then they wait, and wait, and wait until they reach the project deadline and close it out discouraged. This is what happens to more than 60% of projects.

Why? Just because you build it does not necessarily mean backers will come.

Building Community

One of the biggest hurdles to overcome in crowdfunding is that of creating a community, rather than an audience. Marketing classes in school are singularly focused on "reaching your audience" and getting your message across. The average American sees as many as 4,000 ads a day; so many that we have learned to subconsciously ignore them. Billion-dollar corporations pay big bucks just to break through that subconscious roadblock and get the message across to their target audience.

Buy you don't have a billion dollars. If you cannot reach hundreds of thousands with traditional marketing mega-bucks then you need the power of community.

Be warned, building a community is more than just getting people to click that they "Like" your Facebook page. Building a community is about establishing a relationship through interaction and trust. It is about sharing real value.

Communication is the key to building a community. We've all been there. You just put down a big chunk of money for something and now you are wondering if it was a mistake. Buyer's remorse!

You need to contact each of your funders to your project as soon as possible after they donate or invest. Reinforce those ideas that led them to donate or invest and overcome their buyer's remorse. This is most easily done with an auto-respond message that strikes an emotional cord and hits on your key points. If you really want to build community though, aim for a personal call within 24 hours.

It doesn't stop there. Plan a series of contacts that you go through with every funder. Follow the call with an email the next day that addresses any questions (you need to ask them and be listening for any doubts or questions) and reinforces the key points in your project. The longer you can keep that emotional appeal in their mind, the more they will grow to support your project.

After your initial contact and email, give them a few days then send another email asking for a favor. Make it something relatively small like sharing an email with three of their closest friends. The more someone does for your project, the more they share themselves, then the closer they will feel to the project and will make its goals their own.

If you get a rejection to your request or the funder did not follow through with it, ask for something else. Researchers at Stanford found that people are much more likely to say yes to a favor after rejecting an initial request. We have an inner need to be liked and help others. The guilt of rejecting someone not once, but twice is too much for many people.

After a request or two, gauge your supporter's commitment with another phone call. Talk to them about a problem you have been experiencing and ask their advice. You may even go so far as to ask them to help review or revise a detail of the project. Anything to make them feel that they are a part of the project, that they have a level of ownership and a motive to get it funded.

If they are eager to help, they may be ready for a bigger role in the community. Talk to them about how important it is to get "our" project funded and how it will make a difference. Talk with them about how important it is that other people know of the project.

Overcome your natural hesitation to be "pushy." There's no place for it as a small business owner. If you are truly passionate about your company or cause, it will show through and your perseverance will pay off.

Some in your community will become independent marketers and will need less reinforcement or guidance. You'll still need to touch base every once in a while to keep them motivated and involved but the interaction will be minimal to the benefit they will bring. Others in your community will be just as enthusiastic but will need more guidance.

Social Networking

They say that a person needs to see something seven times before it is converted to long-term memory. With social media and the onslaught of virtual requests on the internet, I would bet this number is much higher. That is why you have to make your social networking campaign completely integrated and redundant.

- Update all your personal profiles to include a description of the project and a link that directs to either your project website or directly to the campaign page on the crowdfunding platform.

- Add a button or clickable text signature to your email accounts.

- Consider making a series of YouTube videos that you can post on Facebook and your project website. Make sure you provide links within the video to your campaign.

- Make regular Facebook status updates within your personal profile as well as the project's profile.

- Post information on the Facebook pages of related groups or organizations.

- Comment on blog posts of subjects related to your project and provide a link back to your website or campaign. Make sure your comment is relevant to the blog post or it could be considered as spam.

- Make sure you respond to any comments on your own blog or website.

- Keep updated on any news related to your project and pass it along through your network.

- Consider other social media sites besides Facebook as well, for example: LinkedIn, Pinterest, Twitter, Google+, Instagram, Flickr, Vine, Meetup, Tagged, Ask.fm and Classmates.

Some final thoughts:

- Provide a virtual button to funders that says, "I support project XYZ," and ask them to display it in their email signature and on their social networking pages. This can be a string of text that links to your project page, but a small image works best.

- Depending on the geographical reach of your community, you may be able to meet face-to-face with the most motivated in your group. A personal visit is even more powerful in our world of clicks and likes. Try working your way up from a quick coffee to helping them host a dinner party to reach out to others.

- If you have the ability and budget, a forum on your website can be a giant leap to creating community. This will not only help exchange ideas but will help your community motivate each other with less direction from you.

- Your own budget and how many supporters you need will determine how you build your community. The best method is through regular phone calls and personalized emails but this may not be possible with a small budget and many funders. If your budget supports it, try hiring someone to help make those community contacts but make sure they share your passion for the project.

Step Fifteen:

GET THE BEST BANG FOR YOUR CROWDFUNDING MARKETING

Spending your time on free methods of pre-launch crowdfunding marketing will get you the most bang for your buck but there are still some great ways to get free and inexpensive marketing for your crowdfunding campaign after it has gone live.

But you shouldn't expect your entire crowdfunding marketing strategy to be free. Crowdfunding a business idea or product is just like running a business and budgeting a little to marketing promotion can go a long way. Learn where to put your money down will help you rock out the campaign and beat your goal.

Offline Crowdfunding Marketing

Despite the fact that crowdfunding is an online phenomenon, offline outreach and crowdfunding marketing is still a very effective tool. Even if your campaign does not benefit the local community directly, there is still something to be said for old school marketing ideas.

If you didn't throw a crowdfunding pre-launch party, you need to host one as soon as possible after the launch. Even if you did host a pre-launch, consider hosting another party towards the end of the campaign. After a few weeks of crowdfunding, you should know enough new people to build interest in another event.

Of all the crowdfunding marketing events or advertising you do, the event branded around your own campaign will be the most effective at helping you meet your funding goal. People are there to talk about and be sold on your campaign. Even if they just wanted to get out of the house, there will be that feeling of obligation to at least listen to your pitch. As with the pre-launch, gather a team of enthusiastic supporters before the party to build your strategy:

- Key talking points around the campaign

- What does the campaign mean for different people?

- How to ask for a pledge and how to handle common rejection excuses

- How to ask for non-monetary support like outreach to a group or professional services

Next to the campaign party, conferences and trade shows are the next best thing to a targeted audience. I have talked to campaigns that funded their entire goal from one conference, simply by having a demo model that people could try out. This is why I recommend planning your campaign dates around a large event. After really seeing your product, people can immediately go to the campaign page to lock in their pledge.

Your budget may not allow for booth space but you can still carry a demo model of your product around with you. Without the focus of a formal booth, you will need to actively approach people to talk about your campaign.

- Lead in with your 30-second pitch.

- Ask questions and genuinely get to know who they are and their business or personal needs.

- Ask if you can show them your product or service.

- Emphasize how it is applicable to something you heard them mention.

- Aggressively ask for their support on the campaign and ask for a specific reward level.

- Offer to show them the campaign page on their tablet or phone or offer to open the page on yours.

- Get their business card.

Online Crowdfunding Marketing

The problem with online marketing is a terrifically-low click through rate (CTR) on advertising. Research from Coull.com shows a CTR of just 0.1% for display ads. That means 1,000 people will need to see your ad before one person clicks through to the target.

Social media click-through rates are not much better. Rates on Facebook were 0.5% to 2% while ads on Twitter were as high as three percent. The performance of Twitter ads may be short-lived and it's expected that, as more ads are placed on the site, the effectiveness will fall in line with other media.

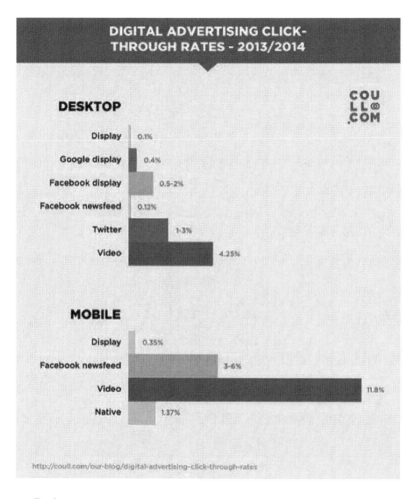

In fact, each one of us sees about 1,700 banner ads each month. Do you remember any of them?

So the question becomes, "How to advertise online without throwing money at it?"

Don't Just Make One Video

Looking at the graphic on advertising effectiveness, the answer to the question should be fairly obvious. Click through rates on video advertising are consistently higher than any other form and as high as 12% on mobile.

Of the different places to spend money on your campaign, I will repeat that video production should be one of the top on your list. You do not need a Hollywood saga but should spend enough for production and editing. The use of video can really take your campaign beyond script and evoke the emotion you need to build community.

Fortunately, video production is one of those things that gets much cheaper in bulk. Getting the professional out to your site may cost a few hundred but once he's out there it may only be a marginal expense to shoot several different scenes. Take advantage of this and draw up at least three videos, each no more than two or three minutes long. You'll need one as your main campaign video but the others can be used to really bring out the story.

For your additional videos:

- **Make it a series**. If you can craft a compelling story and then split it across the series, you might get some serious buy-in as people come back to see successive videos. Your product or service may determine the mood but get creative. Your series does not have to be a factual commercial but could be a thriller-comedy-action saga where your product just happens to feature prominently.

- **Cover different needs or emotions with each**. If you've got several really good selling points to your campaign but they get lost when all included at once, focus on each through a separate video. Odds are better that one of your messages will resonate with viewers.

Beyond the obvious places to upload your video series, there are a couple more that may surprise you. Of course, YouTube should be your first stop followed by Vimeo and Vevo. The three offer paid packages but you should only need the free features.

Beyond images, Flickr is also gaining popularity as a video-hosting site and boasts 16.5 million unique visitors a month. Don't forget to post your videos and share across Facebook as well. The fact that videos are not yet as prevalent across these two sites will help yours stand out and drive traffic back to the crowdfunding campaign.

Paid Advertising

Even on the horrible click-through rate of online advertising, it can find its way into your marketing strategy.

You will need to have a good idea of how your articles are faring on social media. If you do not publish regularly to a blog and then promote through social media, at least try writing up four or five articles related to your campaign.

Measure the reach and social sharing of each article to find out if any do particularly well. Given some feedback from your network, you may even be able to improve on an article with a new title or feature image. The top performing articles in terms of clicks and campaign support will be the ones you want to use for your paid crowdfunding promotion. You already know that these will convert random visitors to higher engagement on a free-sharing basis; they should also do well when promoted.

Besides testing which article to promote, you will also want to test which advertising network to use for your crowdfunding marketing. Start out with a nominal budget across Google, Facebook and Twitter. You can expand the test to other platforms if you like but these three are generally the most popular and cost-effective.

Looking through the results of your test run should give you good ideas of where to focus a higher marketing spend. Beyond the absolute number of visits and clicks, look to how many people were actually converted to campaign backers. You may need to reach out personally to any new backers during those specific days to find out how they became aware of your campaign.

While display advertising is the most popular, paid content performs better and will get more of your message across. Looking through your outreach list of bloggers and influencers, paid content may be the answer if there are any that you just haven't been able to reach otherwise. Blogging or running a highly trafficked website is a business and most offer some kind of content promotion.

Ask for a media packet which will show traffic statistics to the site. The site will likely offer banner advertising but a paid post will be more effective at reaching people. Paid posts are just like regular ones, where either you or the blogger writes an article for publication. Your click-through-rate on content will likely be a little higher compared to display advertising but you should use 1% as a conservative estimate. If a 1% CTR on their website traffic will draw more people than the lower click-through on display advertising at a comparable spend, then it might be something to consider. The best thing about working directly with a website or blogger is that there is always room for negotiation. Don't be afraid to ask for a lower price or a package deal.

Even the United Way has to spend money on marketing and your crowdfunding campaign will likely be no different. Budgeting a little to crowdfunding marketing can save you a lot of time and help reach people that you might not otherwise. Be smart about where you spend and how much you spend on any one resource and there is no reason why promoting your campaign cannot help you meet your crowdfunding goal.

A Word on Crowdfunding Promotion

A whole industry of crowdfunding promotion has evolved from the fact that 60% of crowdfunding campaigns fail to reach their goal but what are you really getting for your money?

Media attention to huge crowdfunding campaign success stories has convinced thousands to jump into online funding before really understanding what it takes to raise money from the crowd. This contributes to the fact that two-thirds of campaigns fail to meet their goals and that 12% never raise anything.

Enter the crowdfunding promotion services and lofty promises to get your message to thousands of bloggers, journalists, influencers and ultimately crowdfunding supporters.

You shop around and decide to try out a seemingly reasonably-priced service that offers high hopes and the potential for your crowdfunding campaign to go viral…and then you hear crickets chirping in the background.

Why are some of these crowdfunding promotion strategies doomed to fail? What really works and what is just a fantasy?

Crowdfunding Promotion: Press Releases

Press releases are probably the most popular crowdfunding promotion service offered online. Why? Because it's easy and can be done at little cost to the service provider.

Crowdfunding service providers promise to blast your press release out to their list of thousands in media, blogging and other online groups.

The results? Take a look at what one campaign owner posted on the internet. I've deleted the name of the service provider for legal reasons.

Analytics	Referrals	Funds	Fulfillment			

		Massive traffic to your campaign through paid			
Campaigner Stats	8 Aug - 21 September	promotion means nothing if it's not targeted.			

Referrer		Referrals	Funders	Contributions
	⇨	5,897	0	$0

Nearly 6,000 referrals to a campaign came from the press release but not a single contribution.

The first problem is that your press release is likely going to the same list used for every crowdfunding campaign. What makes you think a journalist is going to open one particular email about a campaign among the hundreds they may receive every week? Most crowdfunding service providers do nothing to build relationships with people on their lists. As great as your idea is, it isn't going to be news unless you make the effort to reach out and explain why people should be interested.

The second problem with this type of crowdfunding promotion is that the list often has little to do with your topic or your campaign. Just because a journalist has covered crowdfunding before does not mean they want to interview every campaign that gets launched on Kickstarter. An outreach list of 100 people, customized to target a relevant audience, is better than a list of thousands if they are not going to have the slightest care about your campaign.

What about a few of the other promises for crowdfunding press releases?

- Crowdfunding service providers promise to submit your press release to search engines, implying that you could get thousands of visitors from Google and Yahoo. Any page on the internet is available to search engines and service providers really aren't doing much except indexing your page from their website. There is almost no way that you're release is going to get much traffic from search though unless someone searches for the title. Most releases are not long enough and do not include the right factors (backlinks, keyword strength, quality content) to get ranked on the first pages of Google.

- Press releases blasted out to bloggers and other websites carry no real value to the recipients. A blogger that constantly posts spammy press releases to their audience with no regard to quality is going to see their traffic plummet. Blog and website content needs to be engaging and offer something of value to the readers. This is why I ask campaign owners to write about their experience crowdfunding for my readers rather than a simple commercial about their campaign.

Crowdfunding Promotion: Social Media Campaigns

Social media is the Holy Grail of crowdfunding promotion. Where else but Facebook can you reach a potential audience in the billions for free?

Crowdfunding service providers promise to get you hundreds and thousands of followers or to get your message tweeted out to their massive list of crowdfunding enthusiasts.

The problem is, that's not social! Social media is about engaging and interacting with people. Blasting a tweet out to thousands and expecting anyone to care is like walking through an auditorium of people for 30 seconds and expecting Mr. or Mrs. Right to follow you out the door. Most have no interest in your message and the rest are not given enough to find out about it.

Check out the Twitter feed of some of the crowdfunding service providers. What makes you think your message is going to get noticed out of the hundreds tweeted by the company every day?

Worse still is the crowdfunding service providers' claim of an engaged and interested audience in their social followers. Want to know how many of these companies built that huge following for their Twitter or Facebook pages? Do a Google search for "buy Twitter followers" or "buy Facebook likes." I can get 18,000 Twitter "followers" for $15 and 10,000 FB likes for just a little more. It looks great if you are trying to sell services but does nothing for reaching an audience.

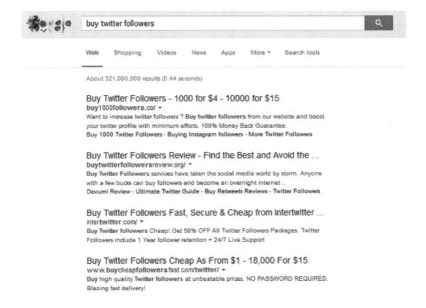

All those fake Facebook likes may actually keep you from getting your message seen by people that really care. Facebook only sends out posts to a portion of the page's follower list. If people from that first group like or share the content, then Facebook sends it out to more of the group. If your message is only received by uninterested followers that are going to do nothing with the post, then it may never reach those few interested followers.

Even the service providers that offer to target and engage social media groups with a message may not be offering much that will convert to funding for your campaign. Check out crowdfunding promotion pages on Facebook or LinkedIn and you'll see post after post of, "Support my Campaign," followed by a link. These posts offer no reason for people to even click through the link. Social media is about being social, duh! You need to actively engage people with questions and give people a reason to be a part of your team.

Crowdfunding promotion has gotten a bad name with the growing list of spammers and false promises but I really believe that you can do promotion correctly and it can help your reach your crowdfunding goal. If you decide to seek crowdfunding services from a third-party, be critical of the offer and the promise of huge traffic to your campaign. Ask questions about the relevance of distribution lists and how the provider will actually drive engagement and interaction with people on the list.

Step Sixteen:

KEEPING YOUR CROWDFUNDING COMMUNITY MOTIVATED

If you've ever launched a crowdfunding campaign, you know of the mid-campaign curse. This is that period usually after the first two weeks but before the last week where crowdfunding pledges and community motivation drops off a cliff.

Even shorter crowdfunding campaigns of 30 days go through this period where people just don't seem to be interested. The community around your campaign has lost its motivation and the drop in daily pledging is absolutely disheartening. It's here that a lot of crowdfunders give up all hope and cancel the campaign.

Check out the Kicktraq graph of daily pledging on Rennick Soholt's Forced Change campaign on Kickstarter. The campaign got off to a strong start with $5,288 pledged over the first two days, nearly 20% of the goal. Then things fell apart and the campaign raised an average of just $247 a day over the next three weeks, not counting three days in which Rennick used one of the strategies below.

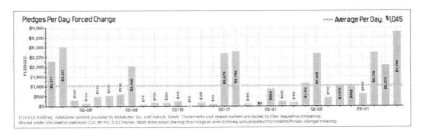

Fortunately, the campaign really got energized towards the end and managed to beat its funding goal by four thousand dollars.

But most campaigns are not so fortunate. Most campaigns fail to build enough support at the end of the campaign and end up missing their funding goal.

So how do you keep your crowdfunding network motivated throughout the campaign?

Keeping your network motivated means understanding the reasons for the mid-campaign curse. Most of these reasons are fairly common across all campaigns so building the solutions into your crowdfunding campaign can help prevent them before they even occur.

The Crowdfunding Campaign Goes Silent

If you've reviewed enough campaigns, you've seen your share of campaigns that have no comments and no updates. You've got to hope that the campaigns are communicating across email and other means but it's probably not the case.

Not only do backers need to know that you are still there, working hard on the campaign, but visitors to the crowdfunding page want to see that you will keep them updated. No one is going to support your campaign if you are going to keep them in the dark.

The solution, update your campaign frequently. Potential updates are:

- Percentages of your goal achieved (20%, 50%, 75%)

- Any news or developments related to your product or service

- Feedback and testimonials on your product or service

- Social network support from influencers or bloggers

One of the biggest problems in crowdfunding campaigns is that people feel there is really nothing new. People get excited around a campaign but can quickly lose that enthusiasm if they don't see progress or new developments.

Don't assume that your community will be checking in on your crowdfunding page regularly. Send your updates through emails, social media and your blog to make sure everyone hears the good news.

I've Already Given Money, What Else is There?

Another hurdle, especially if you haven't built that emotional attachment to your campaign, is that people lose interest after their financial pledge. Backers in it simply for the rewards have gotten what they want and lose interest. Even your close personal network might think their job is over after that initial pledge.

For this, you really need to tap into the other reasons people support crowdfunding campaigns.

- Be a part of something bigger—Make sure supporters know how important they are, not just to you but to the bigger picture. Even if your campaign is for a product or business idea, it serves a need and makes an impact.

- Pride—Make sure to recognize your backers regularly through social media and on your blog. Point out the biggest backers and recognize non-monetary support. Regularly announce largest backers of the day or week.

Work it right and you could get a few backers competing for the recognition.

- Fun—Create mini goals for the week and promise to do something embarrassing or wacky if the goal is reached. Involve backers in the events and make a game of it.

No Reason to Give More

Even without hitting on those emotional reasons to keep the campaign alive, there are a few ways to keep your crowdfunding network motivated.

The Forced Change crowdfunding campaign featured above was able to increase daily pledges by 10 times over the average during three days by finding backers for pledge matches. Find a backer or a group of backers that is willing to match pledges received during a 24-hour period. Update your community at least a few days ahead of the big day and several times throughout the match pledge day.

Stretch goals and rewards are the single best way I have seen to keep a community motivated and can help blow away your crowdfunding goal. The idea is to set your initial funding goal low enough to be fairly easily reached. Then each stretch goal is set well within reach of the previous goal and includes extra rewards. Build a story around each goal and a reason for your community to reach for it. Use regular updates and outreach to motivate backers to get to the next goal.

With a little planning and active communication on your part, you can avoid the mid-campaign crowdfunding curse and beat your funding goal many times over. Use updates to keep your network involved and motivate them to reach for higher funding goals.

Post-Campaign Fulfillment and Community

So you've successfully crowdfunded your big idea and the money is on the way. Now what? Nearly all the blogs and online resources I've seen focus exclusively on running a campaign with little information as to what happens afterwards.

There's only one step in post-campaign crowdfunding but it is just as important as any of the others. Fulfilling your promises and keeping the sense of community for your business will be crucial if you ever want to crowdfund again. Even if you don't plan on crowdfunding in the future, don't miss out on leveraging your hard work into something better.

Step Seventeen:

KEEPING CAMPAIGN PROMISES AND LEVERAGING YOUR COMMUNITY

After the crowdfunding campaign is when the real work begins. Use the momentum and sense of community from a successful crowdfunding campaign to really kick your idea into high gear.

So you've successfully crowdfunded your idea and the money is being dispersed by the platform. Congratulations, you've joined a small but growing list of successful 'crowdpreneurs' and could be on your way to even better things ahead.

But don't think that your job is done after collecting your money. One of the worst things you could do is let all that hard work go to waste by not fulfilling your promises and keeping the momentum going. Not carrying through with your crowdfunding rewards promises might even leave you legally liable.

The State of Washington filed a lawsuit against Altius Management after its Asylum Playing Cards raised more than $25,000 on Kickstarter and failed to send out rewards. The suit is seeking restitution, the state's legal costs and $2,000 for each violation of the Consumer Protection Act.

Besides the monetary loss, Altius Management has lost the loyal support of a community more than 800 strong that could have propelled the company well beyond that initial campaign.

Which makes one of the most important questions in crowdfunding, "How do you manage your crowdfunding campaign after your campaign?"

It's Not a Thank You, It's a Job Well Done!

The first thing you need to do is to reach out to all your supporters and everyone involved in the campaign. Don't thank them for their donation! Congratulate them for being a part of the team and tell them you appreciate all their hard work. The idea, as you'll see throughout your post-crowdfunding steps, is to keep that sense of community alive.

You will need to keep responding to comments and providing updates to your crowdfunding campaign page well after the campaign is closed. Keep everyone updated on the status of production, rewards fulfillment and delivery.

Remember, you're community isn't working on this day-to-day so they can't see the hard work you are doing and progress made. If you stop sending out regular updates, the project goes dark for your community and they will quickly lose interest or get disappointed.

A website or blog can handle a lot of the work and is great for continuing to build that search presence. Leave detailed updates on the blog and then summaries with links back on the crowdfunding campaign page. This has the added bonus of drawing people back to your website and to the rest of your company's message.

Focus on Delivering your Crowdfunding Promises

A growing problem for crowdfunding is non-fulfillment or late delivery of rewards. As crowdfunding grows and more campaigns are successful, a certain number are going to fall behind or just become total busts.

Setting a realistic timeline for production and crowdfunding rewards fulfillment should start in your pre-launch crowdfunding planning. Don't panic if you find yourself going beyond the timeline, it happens to most but you need to be honest and upfront with the community.

Within your campaign updates and on the blog, be completely honest about bugs in the process and even any potential problems you might see coming.

A good problem is having to fulfill way more rewards than expected. The Kickstarter project Ministry of Supply closed its campaign in 2012 beating its initial $30,000 goal by 14-times and being responsible for more than 10-times the rewards they expected. All the logistic partners they had sourced before the campaign were unable to fulfill the orders. They needed new manufacturing, fulfillment, packaging...everything.

The crowdfunders were completely transparent with their nearly 2,800 backers. They outlined the entire supply chain so supporters could see how complex the problem had become.

You know what they found? That backers were actually fine with the delay because they were informed. Backers felt just as successful as the crowdfunders because they had made it all possible. The campaign's problems were their problems because they felt that sense of community.

Whatever you do, resist temptation to start thinking about future campaigns, new products or new features. Stay focused,deliver on your promises and your community will reward you with all the funding you need in the future.

Leverage your Crowdfunding Success

After you've delivered on all your crowdfunding rewards and promises, it's time to really get to work. A successful crowdfunding campaign gives you a ton of credibility and sets the stage for even more funding in the future.

Do not assume that your crowdfunding campaign was a one-time event or project. You've proven your ability and the idea's worth in a market that disappoints nearly two-thirds that launch a campaign. That success took a ton of outreach, research and social work and you do not want to let it go to waste. Even if you only post to your blog once a week, you will be able to conserve a lot of the momentum for when you need it in the future.

Fail to bank that momentum and you'll have to complete the entire process again.

You will definitely want to host a post-campaign party to congratulate everyone and keep that sense of community growing. You do not have to set a mega-budget for the event, it can be set up for next to nothing by partnering with a local establishment and having people pay for their own food or drinks.

It will depend on how much you raised and what you crowdfunded but the money from your campaign is not going to last forever. You will want to start thinking about future sources of funds.

Naturally, another crowdfunding campaign will be an option and much of the work will already be done. You will still want to do additional research, outreach and marketing but your established community is going to make it so much easier this time around.

Depending on where your business or project is at, you might even consider equity crowdfunding. Equity crowdfunding is the process of selling a share ownership in the company to investors, much like has been done for centuries on the stock exchanges. The downside is that you give up some of the control and profits to investors but the upside is that most equity crowdfunding campaigns raise hundreds of thousands and even up into the millions of dollars.

The credibility you gain from a successful crowdfunding project might be able to get your foot in the door of a venture capital or angel investor firm. These companies specialize in funding early-stage companies and helping them grow their sales and profits. They will require a portion of the profits and some control but will offer decades of experience in management and could take your idea to the next level. Before crowdfunding, this was the path for almost all new start-ups and remains a great option for raising money.

Resources

There are plenty of free resources for your crowdfunding campaign that can provide information and guidance. Blogs are a good source of free advice though it may take a while to find the answer to a specific question. Within the crowdfunding universe, there are also plenty of service providers offering varying level of resources and costs.

I cannot make a blanket statement that you should avoid crowdfunding service providers since I count myself as one of them. However, from what I have seen, the quality and attention you will get from a lot of service providers is disappointing and misses the mark. Make sure you ask for references and talk to the service provider about results you can expect before paying too much for detailed service plans.

Most of the resources I've listed below offer free information or services.

Crowdfunding Resources

Kickstarter Creator Handbook I call this one out but most platforms have some kind of educational resource to help you plan and manage your campaign. Spend a little time to read through it to pick up any information specific to the platform that you'll need to know.

Kicktraq is one of my favorite crowdfunding resources. On the site, you will be able to view daily pledges and backers for any Kickstarter campaign as well as social sharing and other information.

BackerKit offers a program to manage and track your rewards and delivery out to backers.

ThunderClap lets you create a profile to gain support from others on the platform. If your profile gains enough support before a deadline then the site posts your campaign to social media sites like Facebook and Twitter.

PitchFuse lets you post your campaign idea and get feedback from the community. The site does not have a ton of traffic but is a good resource for connecting with other crowdfunding campaigns to get feedback.

Crowd101. OK, I had to put in one last shameless plug for the blog. There really is a ton of information on the site and I

am always willing to answer quick questions from readers.

General Resources

Google Drive is a great resource for sharing and collaborating on your campaign with others in the team.

WordPress is the platform on which you will create your blog to build community around your brand.

MailChimp offers a free program for email subscription until you reach 2,000 subscribers.

Tee Launch will print and ship t-shirts directly to your backers.

LaunchRock offers an easy solution to creating a single webpage to pre-launch your campaign and build excitement. If you do not plan on putting together a full blog or website, a landing page is a must.

Eventbrite is a useful website to help you plan and promote your events and meetings.

Buffer is a social media tool that lets you connect and automate your different social accounts. It makes it much easier to schedule social posts or to integrate across accounts.

Made in the USA
San Bernardino, CA
18 February 2016